Martina Piclin
February 1983.

Schizophrenia and madness

Schizophrenia and madness

Andrew Croyden Smith

London
GEORGE ALLEN & UNWIN
Boston   Sydney

George Allen & Unwin (Publishers) Ltd,
40 Museum Street, London WC1A 1LU, UK

George Allen & Unwin (Publishers) Ltd,
Park Lane, Hemel Hempstead, Herts HP2 4TE, UK

Allen & Unwin Inc.,
9 Winchester Terrace, Winchester, Mass 01890, USA

George Allen & Unwin Australia Pty Ltd,
8 Napier Street, North Sydney, NSW 2060, Australia

First published in 1982

British Library Cataloguing in Publication Data

Smith, Andrew Croyden
   Schizophrenia and madness.
1. Schizophrenia
I. Title
616.89′82   RC514

ISBN 0-04-157008-1
ISBN 0-04-157009-X Pbk

Library of Congress Cataloging in Publication Data

Smith, Andrew C.
   Schizophrenia and madness.
Bibliography: p.
Includes index.
1. Schizophrenia.   I. Title.   [DNLM: 1. Schizophrenia.
WM 203 S642a]
RC514.S547 1982   616.89′82   82-11549
ISBN 0-04-147008-1
ISBN 0-04-157009-X (pbk.)

Set in 10 on 11 point Imprint by
Alan Sutton Publishing Limited, Gloucester
and printed in Great Britain by
Biddles Ltd, Guildford, Surrey

Preface

This is not a textbook on schizophrenia for psychiatrists, nor a full account of insanity in society, which would require many volumes. I wanted to write a short account of the major mental illness and the ways of regarding it, for the general reader and for students of social sciences, nursing and medicine.

I have described the patients, the condition and what is known about it from my own knowledge as a psychiatrist, and from research in my own and related professions. However, it is clear that the subject is not purely a medical one, and I discuss widely different viewpoints, using them to make a broad cross-disciplinary formulation of a way to look at schizophrenia.

I have written without technical terms or jargon, hoping to reach any interested reader who might have no specialised knowledge.

I am very grateful for the many improvements suggested by Alan and Patricia Norton, and give my profound thanks to Mrs F. Downing and Mrs J. Bartlett for taking great pains over the typing of the manuscript. Finally, I would like to thank the R. D. Laing Trust for permission to quote from *Knots*; and James MacGibbon, executor, for permission to quote from the work of Stevie Smith.

Andrew Croyden Smith
Greenwich District Hospital
January 1982

Contents

I was much further out than you thought
And not waving but drowning . . .

I was much too far out all my life
And not waving but drowning.
(From *The Collected poems of Stevie Smith*,
London: Allen Lane)

. . .
I have forgotten moon and sun
And songs concluded and undone,
And hope and truth and all things save
The broken wit, the waiting grave.

Where is that mountain I must climb
To gain again some common time,
Not this stayed clock-hand that must be
Some foretaste of eternity?
Where is that task or terror that
Will wake a slow magnificat
From this dead sense, from these dull eyes,
That see no more to Paradise?

There is no night as deep as this
Inevitable mind's abyss,
Where I now dwell with foes alone.
Feather and wing and breathing bone
And blessed creatures come not here,
But the long dead, the aguish fear
Of never breaking from the hold,
Encapsuled, rapt and eras old.

There is no second of escape
As with some forest-wandering ape
Whose sad intelligence may go
So far and never more may grow.
I am enchained most subtly by
A thousand dendrons 'til I die
Or find my mountain, storm and shock
This graven hour and start the clock.

(From Lines written after a nervous breakdown (1).
In *The pure account*, poems by Olive Fraser, collected, selected
and introduced by Helena Shire. Aberdeen: Aberdeen University
Press, 1981.)

1
Introduction

Schizophrenia, the main form of insanity, is treated by psychiatrists and nurses. Madness, a tragic fate, fascinates children, bar-gossips, criminal lawyers, great writers – in fact all of us. To whom should we listen if we want to understand schizophrenia and madness: Shakespeare in *King Lear, Hamlet, Macbeth* and *Othello*; sociologists; or the medical writers of textbooks of psychiatry? Can we learn from all of them?

Over the years, information on insanity has been systematically collected and handed on by doctors entrusted with most of the treatment, including the running of asylums. These alienists and asylum medical officers, whose place has now been taken by psychiatrists, naturally pursued their professional interest in biology, the body and disease when thinking about the nature of schizophrenia. The wiser doctors, since at least the time of Hippocrates in Ancient Greece, have been well aware of the importance of the psychology of each individual patient, and of his place in society in influencing his vulnerability and response to disease. However, biological and clinical evidence of the influence of physical disorder, especially of the brain, on the mind and behaviour has not surprisingly led many to search for subtle physical changes as a basis for schizophrenia.

Clues have been sought everywhere: in chemicals in the urine; fingerprints; electrical wave patterns – not only in the brain but even in the liver; hidden infection by obscure viruses; the changes of ageing in individual cells throughout the body; the secretions of the pineal gland; allergy to certain foods – the list is almost endless. Some curious snippets of information will eventually need to be fitted into the mysterious jigsaw puzzle of what has been discovered, but we do not yet know where. For example, more schizophrenics in the northern hemisphere have birthdays in the early months of the year than would be expected by chance, an unexpected and so far unexplained fact.[69]

Much of the research has yielded negative results, but, in spite of this, the scientific process makes steady advances, and I will be describing what is known about the physical causes in Chapter 6.

Psychiatrists have usually found schizophrenia to resemble an illness, which breaks out in the brain, and has a beginning, a course and an outcome. It always seemed to be rather independent of stress in the patients' lives at the time of the breakdown, so that the standard doctrine in psychiatry until the 1970s laid down that although neuroses such as anxiety, hysteria and many kinds of depression were reactions to personal stress, schizophrenia was not. It was a pathological process, a mental illness.

So it was that when I learnt psychiatry everyone from the humblest citizen to the most profound philosophers and writers believed that people were driven mad by being unable to bear what happened to them – everyone, that was, except psychiatrists, who said it was an inner process, not dependent on life's events, with a cause still unknown but confidently expected to turn out before long to be physical. I always thought that this last view was insufficient and am glad that psychiatry now suggests much more complicated and interesting theories of how schizophrenia arises.

Shakespeare's knowledge of madness was deep, but presumably not wide. Psychiatrists' acquaintance with schizophrenia is wide, but has lacked depth. In our time, those with criticisms of what psychiatrists say and do have been the better writers and held the wider audiences: I am thinking of Laing's The divided self,[110] Goffman's Asylums,[63] and Szasz's The myth of mental illness,[212] standard texts in courses of social studies; and, in the cinema, Family life and One flew over the cuckoo's nest.

Yet there are good reasons why it is the doctors who look after these patients. One reason is that people at large show little sign of wanting other professions to have the responsibility. Another is that the role of the brain in influencing our behaviour is unquestionable. A third reason is that the contemporary medical model of schizophrenia pays full attention to the mysterious trinity in the nature of man: his physical, psychological and social aspects.

Among many books on the subject there have been textbooks for medical students and psychiatrists describing the symptoms and signs, diagnosis and how to organise and carry out treatment; autobiographies; and fictional accounts with varying degrees of verisimilitude. The field has not been free of propaganda for political points of view pressing the claims of particular causes of the condition. Schizophrenia, like cancer, has always attracted odd theorists. There are people who believe it is caused by an allergy to wheat protein, and others who believe that schizophrenics have been driven mad as children by their parents mystifying them. These beliefs are held despite the failure to cure the condition by a change in diet, the presence of schizophrenia in countries where diets are very different, or the fact that people can become schizophrenic alone or in old age. Schizophrenia cannot be caused by modern capitalist society when it occurs in communist China and cases can be found in the literature of the ancient world.

It is in fact a complicated subject that has attracted a vast amount of research, and theories that pay no attention to the rapidly expanding body of well based knowledge do not deserve more than passing attention. I offer the general reader a psychiatrist's survey of schizophrenia in the 1980s.

In the next chapter I give the stories of a selection of real patients, taken at random from those receiving treatment from a psychiatric service now. The stories are all true, only details and initials having been changed to make identification impossible. In Chapter 3, I draw together from these accounts and from psychiatric knowledge and practice the clinical features used in defining the condition. Chapter 4 looks around the world to see if schizophrenia is found in remote areas with cultures very different from our own. Chapter 5 engages in a similar search for schizophrenia in history, selecting for special attention first the ancient world, and then Britain in mediaeval and modern times, and examines especially contemporary accounts and textbooks of medicine. Chapters 6 and 7 recount what is known of the causes of schizophrenia from scientific research, and Chapter 8 is devoted to some critics of the medical point of view, especially those who argue that the illness is best regarded as comprehensible deviant behaviour: as a social problem.

In Chapter 9 I summarise the results of all the earlier chapters in order to formulate the best possible understanding of schizophrenia and madness, given that so many questions remain unanswered. In the final chapter, I describe current approaches to treatment in typical psychiatric services, making no attempt to include fringe varieties which there is no reason to think will last.

Words

A relative, friend or neighbour behaves oddly to the great concern of those around. Often he is 'taken away' to hospital, and the tongues wag. The principal insane affliction that comes to our notice in this way is what the doctors call schizophrenia.

Already I am in difficulty choosing my words, for the subject is a powerful and moving one, with taboo words to be avoided in polite conversation and replaced by euphemisms, as we do with sex. As a psychiatrist, I am at home with the medical term 'schizophrenia', applied to an illness that afflicts and disables many people I see in my working life. It is real enough, so I cannot believe it is a myth.

Yet I never call it a 'disease', reserving that term for its proper meaning, for a process with indubitable bodily disorder or damage. 'Illness' seems to me an entirely appropriate term for a condition that changes and disables people so that they are often unable to look after themselves for the remainder of their lifetime. Schizophrenia will frequently be called an illness in these pages, with no further apology, although I shall discuss whether the 'label' (another tricky word, as we shall see) of a medical name, and inclusion among the illnesses, has been over-applied to the victims by their doctors.

In the last sentence I had to stop myself writing 'patients', my usual word, which I use throughout this book. I sometimes call them victims, because they *are,* and never 'clients', which is popular among some other professions.

I also refer to 'mental' illness frequently, because this has been the customary designation for schizophrenia. It is like an illness in that it has a beginning, course and outcome, although it differs from physical illness because the only definite symptoms and signs are 'mental' ones such as hearing things that are not really there. 'Psychological' is synonymous with 'mental'.

'Insanity' is the layman's and lawyer's formal and polite word for mental illness, and I often use it. In origin it corresponds closely to the concept of illness, because *sanus* is Latin for healthy – hence *'mens sana in corpore sano'.* 'Psychosis' is the psychiatric technical term for mental illness or insanity.

'Madness' is the colloquial term for states of odd behaviour, and is the robust everyday word that polite discourse requires us to avoid. The victim, if our friend, may be asked after as mentally ill or insane, but not as mad, which is rude, and used in everyday parlance to add a feeling of incomprehensibility to an action ('He must be mad to do that'). The word 'madness' is particularly taboo among doctors, with their leaning towards long words and wish to avoid direct talk with their patients. The *Oxford English dictionary* makes the following comment on its use: 'The word has always had some tinge of contempt or disgust, and would now be quite inappropriate in medical use, or in referring to an insane person as the subject of an affliction.' However, as this book is for general readers more than professionals, and as I find that 'madness' has been described throughout history and all over the world, I often use this term to describe the phenomenon I am writing about.

2

Stories

Many accounts of the life histories of schizophrenic patients have been written, including autobiographies and profoundly sympathetic accounts by psychotherapists who came to know their patients exceptionally well. Recent examples include R. D. Laing's *The divided self*,[110] the autobiography *Mary Barnes: two accounts of a journey through madness*,[5] Robert Pirsig's *Zen and the art of motorcycle maintenance*,[162] and Green's *I never promised you a rose garden*.[66] In Chapter 5, I refer to well known accounts from the last century: the cases of Daniel Schreber[186] and Daniel McNaughton.[230]

Such stories exist in sufficient quantity, and I shall not emulate them. They are famous partly because they are vivid and extraordinary, and described profoundly, and bearing this in mind I intend to describe the lives of schizophrenic patients in a different way. The deep picture is well known: I shall sketch the broad one, a representative survey. I shall summarise very briefly the stories of typical schizophrenic patients under the care of one psychiatric service in England at the present time: the old and the young, the bright and the dull, the interesting cases and the less so, the successes and the failures. (Only some of the failures: doctors lose touch with some, and, as the old jibe goes, can bury a few of them. Only some of the successes: they are glad to lose touch with their doctors and get on with their lives.) What is lost in depth of focus on the experience of each patient will be outweighed by the interest of the overall view.

From the past

In the 'long-stay' wards of the mental hospital, there are patients admitted decades ago who have never left, or did so only briefly. Other patients admitted at the same time will have left long ago: they recovered, or their partial disability did not prevent their discharge because they still had homes, families, and some hope of getting and holding a job. Those who remained in hospital did so because they needed psychiatric nursing, had greater difficulties in settlement outside because of additional disabilities such as epilepsy or low intelligence, and were so long improving that they became 'institution-alised' over the years and had no desire to leave, or actually refused to go. There was little effective curative treatment before the mid-1950s.

Mr B. R. was admitted in 1951 at the age of 29. He was a simple young man, a labourer and a loner. He had cut his throat a week before, and then jumped out of a window, and had also tried to strangle himself with his braces. He had been brooding that a state-ment in a comic paper had referred to him and his girl friend, and increasingly felt that there were public comments that he had venereal disease (which he had not). In hospital he was very depressed and indecisive for a long time, and he came to be permanently withdrawn, listening to voices. He said that the wireless was sending him messages made up of arrangements from the first letters of words. 'It's like a divider – I feel divided.' He did jobs in the hospital for a few shillings a week. In 1964 he went for a few months to a rehabilitation hostel, but then returned to the hospital. At the age of 60 he has no com-plaints, is looked after but has no active treatment, works in the laundry, and the hospital is his only conceivable home.

Mr L. P. came in at the age of 28 in 1952, but had been in and out of other mental hospitals since he was 19. He was found by the police at 1 a.m., talking incoherently and ducking his head in a tank of cold water at a petrol filling station. His mother was herself in a mental hospital and he had visited her that day. He was frightened that he would be killed and sent to a gas chamber, interpreting all iron railings as surrounding concentration camps. In hospital he remained grimacing as he listened to imaginary voices, and was perplexed, with a number of vague delusional ideas about Germans and the police. In the following years he always rambled in his speech and never recovered. By the early 1970s he seemed perfectly calm on regular medication, was busy with a hospital job, and vigorously resisted efforts to send him out to a hostel. He relapsed into much worse incoherence when the drugs were stopped to see if they were still needed.

Mr A. T. came in in 1946 at the age of 39, went home again, but returned for good in 1948. He was a loner who used to go to football matches but avoided close contact with people. For several years he did not go out to work and mostly stayed in bed doing nothing, while his invalid mother brought him his meals. He believed there were plots against him and that he was in communion with the stars and the birds. He heard the voices of Princess Margaret, the Duchess of Windsor and famous footballers telling him he was entitled to an income for life. A man called 'Gold' was controlling his mind. A few years later he was still communing with the stars, telling the staff that there was a new star in the sky, which meant that the world belonged to him, and at the same time was writing lucid letters complaining of being still confined in the hospital. In 1958 he started drug treatment with chlorpromazine and recovered. In the 1980s he is perfectly normal, not even apathetically institutionalised, working hard in the hospital stores and emphatic that he does *not* want to retire from them. He relapses when the drugs are stopped. Any change in his routine would be harmful and cruel.

Mr P. S., another single, unskilled labourer, came in in 1952 at the age of 38. He complained of peculiar feelings in his body and a smell from his hands. He was worried about a sexual relationship with his older sister-in-law. He was thought to be no more than highly eccentric and was allowed home, but was readmitted as schizophrenic the next year. He had to be transferred from prison after arrest for assaulting his family and accosting women in the street. He heard voices from an invisible power controlling him and believed that everyone was talking about him and signalling behind his back. He said that the ghost of Frankenstein was inside him. He recovered on the new drugs in 1957 and was discharged in 1965. The following year he was readmitted from a medical ward of a general hospital because he was eccentric, homeless, willing to return to the mental hospital, and accepted by it. He stayed on, repairing shoes for low wages and content to live in the institution.

Miss N. A. was admitted at the age of 25 in 1938. She heard non-existent doorbells, complained of peculiar thoughts, and was giggling, grimacing and impulsively smashing china and glass. She never left the hospital, remaining apathetic, laughing to herself and unable or unwilling to do anything at all. She often stood for long periods in statuesque poses, grimacing and suddenly shouting at no one in particular. Years later she had become quiet, easy to care for, and content, but could not live anywhere except in a mental hospital with tolerant and understanding staff.

Miss L. B. came in in 1933 when she was 26. She was screaming, quoting non-stop from the Bible and said that she was Peter Pan. The period when she shouted and sang and was erratic and mischievous did not last long, and for the succeeding years she was quieter, frowning, and stilted in gait, listening to the voice of the Pope and explaining blandly that she was a cross between Joan of Arc and T.E. Lawrence. She helped the nurses with chores in the ward and did not wish to leave the hospital.

Nowadays

Mr A. R., in his fifties, was married as a young man and had a daughter. After some years the marriage broke up and he went back to live with his mother, who was a grumpy recluse. He worked as an electrician until he was 46, when, after a time of overwork and long hours of duty, he began to feel peculiar. He never worked again. He started reading an enormous number of books on science fiction and the occult, and told his relatives that radiations from space were damaging his manhood and inserting sexual thoughts into his brain. He was sure that his living room was bugged and that special vibrations were beamed on to his armchair. He seldom left the living room, and led a totally separate existence from his mother, each of them a hermit in their own room. Rubbish, broken furniture, stale food, thousands of cigarette ends, hundreds of open books and stacks of newspapers under thick dust accumulated in the room, where, 10 years after stopping work, Mr A. R. sat immobile all day in stained clothes with his knees enveloped in a stinking blanket, thinking about strange influences, and cursing all callers. For nearly 2 years he consented, reluctantly, to have injections of one of the drugs used to relieve schizophrenia, but then he refused this too.

The smell of the house was noticeable to anyone walking up the drive. He came to believe that food delivered regularly by his daughter was poisoned, and he stopped eating. He felt unsafe from radiation in the lavatory so he used a bucket in the same airless, rubbish-filled sitting-room. He never emptied this for himself. In the end, his daughter (who called frequently but uselessly), family doctor, psychiatrist and social worker agreed it was essential to use the mental health legislation to admit him to hospital against his will for treatment. In the admission ward, the nurses found that on his toes the mouldy wool of his socks had merged with gangrenous skin, which came off in a bath, leaving raw areas.

He never explained why he had so neglected himself, saying only that there were reasons and he had minded his own business; other people read books too; and he had never been interested in tidiness. He called his mother a stranger who seemed to be living in the same house. In hospital, he lost his severe eccentricities of speech after a few weeks, appeared to enjoy the comfort, never mentioned his original violent objections to being admitted, and did not ask to go home again for some time. After a few months his house had been cleaned up and he returned to it. Since then he has remained content, looked after himself and has no longer been troubled by delusions.

Mr M. T. came to London from Guyana as a child. He worked as a driver, and as a young man he married and had children. When he was in his early twenties he stopped work and started to read books on black magic. He was often suspicious that he was being poisoned. His marriage broke up, and for 2 years he lived alone. He was known to the neighbours as very abnormal, suspicious, and prone to accuse them of interfering with his doormat, dustbins and milk. He practised black magic alone in his house, and sometimes exorcised spirits in the garden, naked.

He created disturbances in the street several times, shouting that he was the Redeemer, and commander-in-chief of a vast personal devil-navy of black men who would take over the world. The police always took him to psychiatric units, from which he absconded at once. In the end he was remanded in prison, and because he remained deluded in this grandiose way, believed all his food had been poisoned and had, in fact, suffered from untreated schizophrenia for 3 years, was moved to hospital for treatment.

In hospital, he rarely said anything abnormal but behaved as if the food were poisoned. During many months of difficulty in finding him somewhere to live he was content to work in the hospital factory. When he went out to live in a bachelor flat he did not install a cooker despite a grant for the purpose, and never went through the rudiments of claiming his benefits from the social security authorities, while alleging they were swindling him. He hit workmen who politely knocked on his door, and set up a mirror and chair so that he could observe the approach of possible intruders. Pugnaciously he explained that all further interference from freemasons would be repulsed as he resented all their plots and efforts to get him out. He had said repeatedly, but never elaborated although he was often asked to do so, that he was not a Catholic but a 'cosmic'. He refused all official contact and all medication. He was persuaded to return to hospital where he rapidly became content again, although he used to say that he wanted to go out to a flat of his own if only he were not interfered with.

Mrs S. J., originally from Poland, was widowed when she was 40 and her children were still at school. They were in the care of the council for long periods, and she usually lived alone in an immaculate flat, becoming more and more preoccupied with her belief that in some mysterious way she was married to the Prince of Wales. She collected cuttings and books about him and believed that newspapers and television programmes made oblique references to his affection for her. Once she caused a commotion at London Airport, invading the VIP lounge and saying she had come to start her Royal Tour. Another time she ordered a pantechnicon, had her luggage packed in it, and gave the destination 'Buckingham Palace'. She did not pay rent, because Royal personages have no need to, and believed that her consort would send for her sometime. She stole from shops and when caught said, 'Send the bill to my husband,' that is, the Prince of Wales. She decided that a neighbour was harbouring him in her house, and banged on the front door night and day demanding that she bring out the Prince from his hiding-place. All the while she was cheerful, unconcerned, and utterly unwilling to behave differently. Sometimes she agreed to take medication, sometimes she did not. She was the same during her periods in hospital as she was in her own home.

Mr P. A.'s parents were graduates, and he and the other children did well at school. Peter was remembered by the masters for asking original and thoughtful questions. In retrospect, the first known peculiarity of his language was when at the age of 16 he wrote and crossed out, in a questionnaire on careers: 'I want to study immaterial chemistry'. However, he secured a place at university, and everyone was surprised when, within a week of the beginning of his first term, he stayed in his room in a trance night and day, causing the tutors to regard him as breaking down. They sent him to a psychiatrist. He went home, missed appointments, and saw no doctor for a whole year, sitting indoors frowning, listening to imaginary voices and brooding over the political manipulations that he believed had been perpetrated on him. Later he went one day to a casualty department saying that his brain needed checking because it was not functioning correctly. During a long stay at the mental hospital, he was always reticent, smiling enigmatically as he indulgently tolerated 'experiments' on him. He believed he was a political casualty. 'You say I had a breakdown at university. I say a crime was committed on me there as part of an experiment.' No physical or psychological treatment helped, and he went home to live with his mother and successful sisters, reading the novels of Hermann Hesse right through 20 times, staying up most of the night and in bed all day, making no friends, showing interest in neither work nor education, and becoming a well-known local eccentric. His father, devoutly religious, with an interest in psychology, wondered whether his latest state should be regarded as his 'authentic' self, more than the bright schoolboy and potential undergraduate. I thought that schizophrenia had destroyed a young man's sanity and his promise, with no compensatory advantages, although I was not unaware of the pungency of the insane man's comments on society when he said, 'It feels as though special interest groups are warring for control of my mind.'

Mrs D. T. had been married and then separated, bringing up a daughter with whom she had a barbed relationship. Mrs D. T. was in her sixties, a pugnacious, obstinate, and latterly lonely embittered person. She lived alone.

She hated her flat and believed that she was surrounded by Nazis who were annoying her by making noises to force her to leave, and who released rats and gases into the bedroom – animals which, she emphasised, she frequently saw, and gases which she actually smelt. She jumped from the first-floor window and broke both ankles. After a year of treatment in hospital her legs were better and she had recovered from the schizophrenic symptoms. However, she was still difficult to get on with, could not fit into an old people's home, probably because she was deliberately obstructive, and, although she no longer had any schizophrenic symptoms, had to settle in the ward of a mental hospital because she could not live anywhere else.

Mr T. I. was admitted to the psychiatric ward when he was 24. He had been flown home from the mental hospital in Santiago, Chile, as soon as he was fit to be transferred to London. He was deep in thought and lost to the world for much of the time, frowning, and preoccupied with the imaginary voices he could hear. He said that they were the voices of two people, unknown to him, discussing him in a running commentary, predicting all his movements with uncanny accuracy. He was certain that there was a communist conspiracy to brain-wash him by intricate, remotely controlled means, but he could not say how, originally, he came to be convinced of this. He saw strange and extremely important meanings in simple actions around him: when I crossed my legs he said, 'I see: that's it then,' meaning that I had transmitted an important signal, and he appeared to be puzzling out the dire meanings of the sounds of cars passing, and the shapes of clouds in the sky.

One day he lay in bed in a peculiar position, partially curled up, but looking very awkward and uncomfortable. Eventually he said that he lay in that way because he was 'a prawn'. Asked to explain further, he said that he felt as though there were political machinations directed against him in which he was but a pawn, 'with an R in it, for Russia'.

He was the only child of a dry, slightly remote mathematician of left-wing opinions and his wife, who had died when Mr T. I. was a baby. Later in childhood he had been brought up by an aunt, with whom he had been the best of friends. At university he read social studies and then proceeded to social work training.

There had been a period of work in a children's home when he had worried over the plight of the homeless children abandoned by their parents, and had at the same time been working very long hours with unaccustomed heavy responsibility. For a few days he had been unable to sleep and had caused concern to his colleagues by talking to himself and appearing withdrawn. He subsequently said that in his room at night he could 'hear' the voices of the children, even the small babies, talking to him and telling him how unhappy they were. He was sent away on holiday, and rapidly recovered.

He continued with his studies, and was active in communist politics at the university. The events leading up to the severe breakdown started when he went on holiday to Chile. He had a whirlwind and deeply affecting sexual affaire while there, and he was sleeping little and drinking far too much. His girlfriend jilted him heartlessly, and exactly at that time the right-wing coup occurred, with shooting and tanks in the streets. It was evidently all too much for him and he became deluded, hallucinated and disordered in his processes of thinking in the way just described. The staff in the hotel reported his odd behaviour, and he was admitted to the local mental hospital whence he was sent back to London.

The hospital staff tried to build rapport and understand his experiences as he recounted them, and he was treated with drugs and with electrical convulsive therapy. He improved day by day, and was only in hospital for 5 weeks.

Afterwards, he was not questioned closely about his interpretation of his nightmarish experiences because it was thought inadvisable to draw attention to them, but he had probably regained almost full insight into their abnormality. Some of them he had forgotten; none of them did he seem to wish to recall or discuss.

He came off the prescribed medication, saw no doctor or other adviser, and proceeded with his life as before. He had friends and sexual relationships, and pursued his career. He qualified as a social worker, and worked in a post of considerable responsibility. Two years after the last illness he again became disturbed, listening to imaginary voices, and feeling watched and persecuted. As had happened before, he was worried over the suffering of the children he met at work, and was involved with a woman who gave him up.

He was admitted to hospital again, treated with drugs and an understanding milieu, and appeared to recover. Unfortunately, discharge was followed by rapid relapse into delusions and hallucinations and he came back to hospital, brought by alarmed friends. Electrical treatment was added to the incompletely effective medication, and in 3 weeks he recovered completely. For 8 years he has remained completely well mentally, pursuing a responsible and independent professional career without difficulty. He takes a small dose of medicine daily as a protection against relapse, he and his psychiatrist agreeing that this is advisable.

Mrs B. D., originally from Jamaica, was 26 years old when she was ill for the first time. She had given birth to her second child 2 months before and had then gone on holiday. While away she felt that the names of the characters in a television programme had special meanings for her, and that there was a mysterious connection with the logbook of her husband's car. Before long, names on advertisements in the street were all coincidences and signals for her. She said she was still getting strange meanings and messages when a psychiatrist examined her. She could not say where they came from, and was struggling to concentrate. Sometimes she became stuck in mid-sentence.

Her mother was in contact with her; her father had died when she was 7. She left school at 16 and went to teacher training college, but left at 18, without completing the course. Her marriage was not happy. After the birth of the older child she had felt for 2 days that people were talking about her, but the feeling had then passed.

The abnormal feelings after the second childbirth remitted within a week of her starting drug treatment, and she did not see a doctor for 3 years.

Then she went to her general practitioner because she was convinced that a needle had been lodged in her eye since childhood, despite X-ray pictures proving that this was not possible. Her husband now said that she was very strange and withdrawn and had not been normal for the whole 3 years. She said, 'I recoil on certain facts of my childhood – when my husband hits me.' She was evasive about the return of strange meanings. She had been telling her priest peculiar stories about her past and the needle in her eye. She and her husband had gone to a Marriage Guidance counsellor, a psychiatrist, who had said she was mentally ill, and should be treated for that first.

She refused help, but at home was laughing and crying to herself, and writing peculiar letters about her past to public figures whom she had seen on television, calling them to bear witness as to the truth about her origins. She continued to be preoccupied with the imaginary needle, and started maintaining that she had been married in infancy at the age of 7 months. Her disturbed state was rapidly getting worse without treatment, and the children were unsafe and frightened. She absolutely denied abnormality and said her husband was the ill person. She was admitted to hospital against her will on an order under the Mental Health Act.

She recounted many delusions, and her language employed words in unusual ways, akin to malapropisms but nevertheless conveying her meaning trenchantly. 'I'm suffering from abject recall'; 'my marriage is licentious bigamy'; 'I've had dichotomy on a number of occasions.'

She said that Fidel Castro was her half-brother, that she was registered as a Cuban citizen at several embassies (she was, in fact, entirely British), that she had qualified as a surgeon 'by stipulation under various names' ('proving' this with a scrap of irrelevant paper), and that she had (invisible) 'police patches' on her fingers (her father had been a policeman).

She refused drug treatment for a long time, but in the end reluctantly agreed, whereupon the abnormalities started to diminish. During the past 5 years she has been out of hospital nearly all the time, bringing up her family, living with her husband and sometimes holding a full-time job. She has also been on regular injections of medication, to which she is very reluctant to agree. Several times she has insisted on stopping them, and has within a few months become bizarre again and unable to live outside hospital. Treatment is then re-established and she gets home within a few weeks. Even at her best she is peculiar and probably retains her odd beliefs below the surface of her mind. It seems as though treatment helps her illness considerably.

However, there are also other ways of looking at such a story. Some have not regarded it as the account of an illness. Laing, in *The divided self*,[110] says that some schizophrenics like her decide to 'play at being sane'. If insanity is, from one point of view, a flight from the outer world into the private inner one, an alienation, then her cure may be a reluctant capitulation to what is required of her in her workaday sane existence. She has not said in which state she is happier, but some patients do. The choice falls nearly always on sanity, but occasionally it does not.

3

The condition

In this chapter I describe the usual symptoms and signs of the schizophrenic condition, what the patients say they experience, and how they behave. This is familiar material in textbooks of psychiatry, which have a chapter on schizophrenia and delineate its 'clinical features'. With due attention to the patients' experiences, and quotations from them, the accounts are nevertheless 'clinical' and external, a matter of dispassionate observation, teaching doctors how to recognise schizophrenia and distinguish it from other conditions requiring different forms of treatment and intervention. What is missing in most textbook accounts is any deep understanding of how the patient's inner life feels to him, but this has been supplied *par excellence* by Laing among psychiatrists,[110] and by autobiographical accounts from patients who have recovered.[5,66,162,186]

These accounts, because of their authenticity and vividness, have been very influential, but because there are few of them they have tended to mould the general view of schizophrenic patients in an unrepresentative way. The most obvious example of this bias is the lack of autobiographical accounts from inarticulate and unintelligent patients. Also, we hear only about the fortunate patients who recover to sanity to tell the tale. Therefore, I unashamedly return in this chapter to a general survey of the features of the schizophrenic illness as known to psychiatrists from their patients, so that the condition as a whole is before us as it was in the stories of the preceding chapter, before we embark later upon an examination of its causes and nature.

Disorder of thinking and language

A disturbance of the process of thinking, and hence of its expression in language, is manifest in most cases of schizophrenia. In severe degree it amounts to a complete disruption, and language becomes an almost formless jumble, the so-called 'word salad'. Sometimes a stream of invented fragments takes the place of words. In more mild cases, the disturbances of clarity, logic and meaning are more subtle, and hard to describe. It is easier to illustrate them, and I have given some examples in the stories of Mr P. A., Mr T. I. and Mrs B. D. in the preceding chapter.

Meaning is changed and becomes less sharp. Sentences tend to take on an abstract quality beyond that of normal discourse on abstract subjects, and it may be found that long speeches transmit hardly any information, although the effect is different from a normal person's evasiveness. The result has sometimes been characterised in textbooks as 'woolly' and 'pseudophilosophical'.

Ronald, in a ward discussion among patients, announced that 'Analogy is doing different things by imaginary methods.' The meanings of different words can be telescoped together to form unique idiosyncratic creations understood only by the patient, if indeed they are understood even by him, and sometimes new words, neologisms, are coined. Meaning is communicated; but it is bizarre meaning, and is imparted in highly unusual ways. Sometimes the effect is vivid, memorable, haunting, like poetry; sometimes it is more like a malapropism.

Examples of this include the statement by Mr T. I. that he felt like a prawn because of the Russian involvement in his being a pawn. Mrs B. D. referred to herself as having 'abject recall' about her childhood. No doubt this includes an element of malapropism in place of 'object', as well as overtones of feeling 'abject' in her disturbed state. Another patient referred to his signature as his 'significance'. The incorrect use of a word like this, a use nevertheless pregnant with wry meanings, is common: the same patient referred to some cartoon characters he had painted as 'acknowledgeable to us as human'. Sometimes form and cadence are correct, but the remark has no meaning: 'Should I return in my absence, kindly detain me till I come back.'

Laing's patient, Julie, who was allowed no individuality by her mother, was dressed as a lifeless, pretty doll, and had been in a mental hospital for 9 years, believed she was a 'tolled bell'. This was interpreted by Laing as deriving from feeling a 'told belle'.[117] Another of his patients spoke of being surrounded by 'insinuendoes'. Mrs B. D. called her marriage 'licentious bigamy'. Sometimes the patient in a flight of fancy may attempt a grand synthesis, as did the engineer who thought he had solved the riddle that had baffled Einstein in his later years, and had found the 'cosmological constant'.

He derived this by inscrutable means from connections which he claimed to detect between events on 'the left and right hemispheres of this planet', 'intergalactic spin in the Milky Way', a cycle of 66.6 years between major wars, 'a simple triploid harmonic motion', and a scheme which attributed the power struggle between the sexes to dominant (X) and submissive (x) sex chromosomes.

Laing says of schizophrenics and their difficulties with thinking and language: 'Their ruminations are unsuccessful and tragically unrecognized efforts to try to get these things straight. They are themselves confused and cannot be expected to understand what they are groping towards. Their efforts at neologism, amendments of syntax, queer information, splitting of words, even syllables, and equivalent operations applied to the whole non-verbal "language" of expression and gesture, require to be re-evaluated, and much further research is required into the original system of communication to which they were first exposed.'[109] The obscurity of expression is sometimes used as a smokescreen in which to hide from or mock those around: 'A good deal of schizophrenia is simply nonsense red-herring speech, prolonged filibustering to throw dangerous people off the scent, to create boredom and futility in others.'[116] In mild forms, it shades off into a highly abstract style that minimises the chance of being pinned down as having said anything definite, although the bones of the message show through. Christopher said, 'I felt unable to make sense of . . . find a way out of . . . my inability to communicate . . . no basically satisfying sense of communicating that I could relate to my present feeling of miserableness . . . I have so much trouble piecing together the strands of my imagination or information that my intelligence receives, perhaps, that my will – I don't think my will has that much control over my imagination . . . the expression, the co-ordination of expression in my imagination – I can't remember what I've just said as a paragraph . . . [you gave up at another college?] . . . couldn't relate it to my life except as a slightly masochistic gesture: I didn't like it . . . I can't make sense of the immediacy of the potential of what I've been led to believe is the potential seriousness of . . . of occurrences [Is that clear?] . . . A bit cryptic . . . does it make sense to you?'

Hallucinations

Every schoolboy knows that talking to yourself is a sign of madness, and it is true that listening to imaginary voices and muttering (or occasionally shouting) replies to them is typical of schizophrenia. Auditory hallucinations of voices can be simple or complex, tentative or certain, cheering or tormenting, incidental or utterly preoccupying. In the beginning the patient may hear thuds and indistinct noises when he is alone in quiet surroundings, and he attends more and more vigilantly to these sounds. Eventually the sounds are heard to be words of comment or command. Real sounds in the surroundings are heard as voices, the patient attending sharply, expecting them to have significance for himself. So, a dripping tap is heard as saying, 'queer, queer, queer' – insistently reminding him of his fears that some people regard him as homosexual. People talking in the corridor, only audible as the muffled sound of human voices, are heard in his inner ear as voices discussing him clearly.

Hallucinatory voices occur in mental illnesses other than schizophrenia, but usually in a fragmentary fashion with isolated words, and sometimes they occur in physical illness when the patient is delirious. Hallucinations of complex absorbing conversations in a patient who is alert and physically fit are typical of schizophrenia, however, especially if they take the form of several voices discussing the patient's thoughts and actions in a running commentary: 'Now he's walking down the road; now he's reached the corner and he's wondering which way to turn; now he's looking at that girl's legs, the filthy so-and-so.'

Hallucinations also occur visually ('seeing things'; 'visions'), and as experiences of smells, tastes and sensations from the skin that are not in fact true perceptions of stimuli impinging on the sense organs from the outside environment.

Delusions

The concept of delusion, typical of but not confined to schizophrenia, is hard to define.[206] Yet despite blurred edges and borderline cases there is usually no real doubt whether someone is deluded or not. The standard definition runs: a delusion is a belief that is in fact untrue but is held unshakably in the face of evidence to the contrary, and that cannot be explained as allowable within the normal limits of the patient's cultural milieu. We must examine the component parts of this definition closely.

The delusion is a *belief* – that is, it is not a feeling, an emotion or a perception. The statement of the belief may be implicit, but that it is a belief is clear – schizophrenic patients believe that they are persecuted, watched, hypnotised against their will, and interfered with. They believe that they are very important people, related to the Royal Family, a reincarnation of Jesus, or the Virgin Mary about to give immaculate birth. They may believe that they have made great discoveries, as did the man who wrote about the 'cosmological constant'. They may be convinced that their wives are secretly copulating with strange men in the kitchen during the night before creeping furtively up to bed again.

The delusional beliefs are untrue in fact. Here already the definition begins to be unsatisfactory when scrutinised closely. Whereas it may be clear beyond doubt that in the literal sense this man is not Jesus, this woman is not pregnant and the other man is not a victim of poison gas being pumped into his house by neighbours, other beliefs may not be so readily tested against the touchstone of factual truth. It is not so self-evident that the engineer has not discovered the 'cosmological constant'. What of quasi-religious beliefs such as those of the man who avers that he has had a message from God and since then knows that he is sent as an anti-Messiah to save the world from Christianity and lead it back to devil-worship? What are the criteria of factual truth in religious statements?

If factual truth is crucial, then an anomalous situation may arise with the delusions of the morbidly jealous man concerning his wife's infidelity. As we have defined the concept of delusions so far, he will be deluded if he is certain of her infidelity while she is, in fact, faithful. If she then becomes secretly unfaithful to him (not a rare event in the destructive atmosphere of such a marriage), he can no longer be regarded as deluded, according to the definition so far discussed. Yet his state of mind has not altered – events elsewhere have changed, unbeknown to him. Clearly the definition is faulty in this respect, and we shall return to this point in a moment.

The belief must be held unshakably in the face of evidence to the contrary. However, we are all pig-headed at times and fail to give up beliefs under attack. The delusion is not merely a strongly held view: it is absolutely held as part of the personality, a conviction, so that giving it up is not merely intolerable but inconceivable. In this it resembles a religious belief: for example, the Christian holds unfalteringly that God is omnipotent and infinitely good, in the face of the contrary 'evidence' of the atheist that the world is full of preventable suffering. His belief is not shaken by evidence, which may, in fact, be regarded as irrelevant: Cardinal Newman said, 'Ten thousand difficulties do not make one doubt'[157]; Tertullian, *Certum est quia impossibile est'* ('It is certain because it is impossible').[218] This is remarkably similar to the position of the deluded schizophrenic, who holds his delusion in the face of, and regardless of, all evidence. He tests evidence against the solid-rock touchstone of the delusion – supportive evidence is interesting, contrary evidence is, for the very reason of its contrariness, to be rejected (perhaps it was mistaken, perjured, part of a conspiracy, only a façade of false pretences and not what it seemed). This is the key to the paradox of the man with delusions of infidelity whose wife becomes secretly unfaithful. The belief is a delusion because of the characteristic way in which it is held with certainty, before the evidence and not depending on it. This characteristic certainty of the delusion is therefore more central to the definition than its untruth.

The sheer intensity of non-rational beliefs at times is described by William James in *The varieties of religious experience:*

> If you have intuitions at all, they come from a deeper level of your nature than the loquacious level which rationalism inhabits. Your whole subconscious life, your impulses, your faiths, your needs, your divinations, have prepared the premises, of which your consciousness now feels the weight of the result; and something in you absolutely *knows* that the result must be truer than any logic-chopping rationalistic talk, however clever, that may contradict it.[92]

In fact, 'The heart has its reasons which reason knows nothing of' (Pascal).[160]

The delusion plays a part in the patient's life analogous to that of religious belief – it makes sense for the patient of an area of his experience, and brings order out of chaos. After describing the mystifying communications in the families of these patients, Laing makes this point: 'The person caught within such a muddle does not know whether he is coming or going: in these circumstances what we call psychosis is often a desperate effort to hold on to something, and it is not surprising in the circumstances that the something may be what we call "delusions".'[109] So terrifying must chaos be, that a delusion, once it has crystallised out of it, can never thereafter dissolve again. When, therefore, the patient suddenly realises, in the blinding flash of awareness of significance that often occurs at the beginning of delusion-formation, that everyone around him is participating in a masquerade, signalling about him and transmitting messages to agents who have a brain-influencing ray-gun that drives him to be homosexual against his will, a turning-point is reached and he may be relieved. The systematic persecution implies that he must be an important person, it accounts for his setbacks in life, and it frees him of responsibility for the resisted and rejected wayward desires he has felt. That is a great deal to explain in the twinkling of an eye, and such a belief is not given up, but becomes part of the whole person and his life thereafter.

The similarity between these experiences, often banal but sometimes more nearly poetic or sublime, and religious conversions will be clear to the reader.

Distinguishing them is not easy. George Fox, the founder of the Quakers, wandered through England responding to the commands of God, which he heard as a voice, to preach fearlessly and publicly wherever he went on the sinfulness and hypocrisy of the world. William James reminds us that Fox was regarded as a remarkably impressive spiritual reformer wherever he went. James uses the case, together with that of St Paul, to lambast the medical point of view that reduces great experiences to the status of disease: 'Medical materialism finishes up St Paul by calling his vision on the road to Damascus a discharging lesion of the occipital cortex, he being an epileptic . . . George Fox's discontent with the shams of his age, and his pining for spiritual veracity, it treats as a symptom of a disordered colon.'[91]

Great men will not fit well into a schizophrenic category if it is an automatic diminution of their achievement and an attribution of 'madness', of unsound mind. Yet there is a continuum from the sublime nature and results of the experiences of Fox and St Paul to the sudden delusions of special meaning of our less gifted patients. The *form* of the experience seems to be similar, but, in the latter, the content has become banal, and perhaps society's response has been different. Angels struggle for the soul of St John of the Cross and St Teresa of Avila, while the following is the story of a recent patient:

> The twenty-three-year-old daughter of a professional man had just left university, where she had obtained honours in foreign languages, and was preparing to apply for the post of translator and confidential secretary at a branch of the United Nations Organis-ation. She began to develop doubts about her religious position (her family were sincere but not particularly strict Roman Catholics) and to fear that she might have committed a sin against the Holy Ghost, for which she and the devil were personally and jointly responsible to God. She heard God's voice reprimanding the devil for his part in the affair, and telling him that his last chance of being received back in Heaven had gone.
>
> Evidence of this cosmic battle for her soul began to grow around her. Riding in a motor car with her parents, she saw the car over-taken by blindfolded motor cyclists who shot invisible rays into the car from pistols. (Later she was able to identify this part of her hallucinatory experiences as related to a Cocteau film *(Orphée)* she had previously seen.) Admitted to hospital at her father's urgent request, through her family doctor, she said she had the obligation of sacrificing herself to save the devil, who was after all only Michael, the fallen Archangel. She refused treatment, pursed up her face and mouth for much of the day, and tried to pull out her own hair. She was eventually persuaded to accept treatment . . . She recovered from all her symptoms and was restored to normal health in five months.[209]

Mr P. A. said, 'It feels as though interest groups are getting at each other through me'; another man called John realised that he was 'the main psychological cover for the Queen' (a cryptic statement; oft-repeated, never amplified); and the engineer discovered the 'cosmological constant'.

The correspondence is that religion may begin with conversion, a dramatic experience of the most profound meaning in which all falls into place (the scales fall from the eyes), and schizophrenia similarly has the primary delusional experience. In both religion and schizophrenia, some believers act as if every detail of their belief were literally true (rare Christians; some schizophrenics who complain to the police about their supposed victimisation), others do not (many nominal Christians; schizophrenics who 'believe' that they are omnipotent, but live passively in mental hospital).

Unfortunately, the clarity of the definition of delusion is blurred by the inevitable proviso that the belief must be unexpected in the patient's culture. The above brief consideration of the similarity between religious and delusional beliefs shows the need for this proviso. Minority religions may be associated with extreme beliefs thought to be bizarre by outsiders, and the same may apply to beliefs in folk-lore, magical practices or politics. Assessment of curious beliefs to decide whether they must be classified as delusional thus requires detailed knowledge of the milieu. If a patient tells me that he believes he is in constant communication with the spirit voice of his departed mother from beyond the grave, this will have very different implications if he is a member of a spiritualist sect, than if he is known to be a no-nonsense rationalist with no interest in such matters. When Pentecostal West Indians or Indian Sikhs consult me in mental illness, I see if their religious beliefs are normal or eccentric by consulting the family or elders of the church before assessing the significance of what is being said to me.

Kräupl Taylor[216] points out that part of the definition of delusions is that they are *preoccupying* to the patient, and that they are *idiosyncratic*. Many people's religious or more banal eccentric beliefs, for example a tenaciously held conviction, in the face of the evidence, that swinging a gold ring over a pregnant mother's abdomen can be used to predict the sex of the unborn child, that human vampires exist, or that flying saucers have been seen landing in our time, may fulfil the other criteria of delusions, but they are held by some normal people and are unimportant to their lives, being concerned with inessential topics. These are not delusional, for the disturbed beliefs of the deluded patients are different, being preoccupying, forming a major feature in the foreground of their struggle through life, frequently mentioned, and all-important.

The delusional belief or system of beliefs is idiosyncratic – it is a unique creation of that patient, whereas religions and eccentric trivial beliefs in folk-lore and related fields are essentially group phenomena. Every devotee of a religion has roughly the same beliefs, although here, too, every man has his own version of the common dogma. The schizophrenic's delusional religion is unique – no one else believes anything remotely like what Mr T. I. believed (that he was a prawn); what Mrs B. D. believed (that she had qualified in medicine by stipulation); or what John believed, in his preoccupying reiterated statement that he was 'the main psychological cover for the Queen'.

We must consider what this means so far. Perhaps there are no strong boundaries between the accepted religions and schizophrenic delusional systems. Perhaps the delusions are pathological and stunted developments of that faculty that derives meaning and comfort from systems of belief, or, from the sociological point of view, perhaps they are deviant personal religions, labelled as being beyond the range of the permitted 'normal'. William James makes this point trenchantly in discussing the cultural unacceptability of idiosyncrasy and uniqueness, and what in the religious context is called heterodoxy:

A genuine first-hand religious experience like this [George Fox's] is bound to be a heterodoxy to its witnesses, the prophet appearing as a mere lonely madman. If his doctrine prove contagious enough to spread to any others, it becomes a definite and labelled heresy. But if it then still prove contagious enough to triumph over persecution it becomes itself an orthodoxy; and when a religion has become an orthodoxy, its day of inwardness is over: the spring is dry; the faithful live at second hand exclusively and stone the prophets in their turn.[93]

Characteristic experiences

In his book *Clinical psychopathology,* Kurt Schneider[185] put forward a list of characteristic phenomena that confirm the diagnosis of schizophrenia and exclude the possibility that the patient is suffering from severe depression, mania or less severe neurotic disturbances. Even these characteristic phenomena, however, sometimes occur in states of ordinary disturbance of the brain. This means that they may be seen in patients who are, or recently have been, physically ill, with clouding of the normal clarity of consciousness by, for example, epilepsy, alcoholism, addiction to amphetamine, or other disorder of the brain. In the absence of these cerebral illnesses, which are commonly recognised in medicine and would take priority of diagnosis, Schneider's 'First-rank symptoms' are taken by most psychiatrists to be quintessentially schizophrenic. They are:

(1)   The experience in which the patient hears his own thoughts spoken aloud as he thinks them (which leads to statements by the patient, often in anger and bewilderment, that other people know what he is thinking before he thinks it. He talks of mysterious thought-reading processes).

(2)   The hearing of hallucinatory voices in dialogue, usually discussing or arguing about the patient.

(3)   The hearing of hallucinatory voices that form a running commentary on the patient's actions.

(4)   The experience of the body being influenced extraneously (which leads to statements that the patient is being hypnotised, is a robot, or is manipulated by uncanny powers – perhaps black magic, or from outer space or the secret service).

(5)   The experience of thoughts being withdrawn from the mind or otherwise influenced (which leads to statements that he is, again, hypnotised by telepathy, or somehow persecuted by malign and mysterious mechanisms).

(6)   The experience of thoughts that are not felt to be his own. This is termed 'thought insertion' by psychiatrists; the patient complains of some external agency imposing the thoughts, by varied means, upon his passive mind.

(7)   The experience of feeling his thoughts broadcast directly from his mind to the outside world (which lies behind statements by the patient that his thoughts seem to appear in television and radio broadcasts at the time that he is thinking them).

(8)   All experiences of being influenced and made to be a passive victim in the field of emotion, drive and willpower. (The patient complains that he is 'made' to feel his emotions. His willpower has been taken away and replaced by a devilish or monstrous incubus that drives him as if he were a mindless robot, and he feels therefore not responsible for the actions of his body.)

(9)   Delusional perception. I shall quote the description used by Mellor: 'Schneider described the delusional perception as a two-stage phenomenon. The delusion arises from a perception which to the patient possesses all the properties of a normal perception, and which he acknowledges would be regarded as such by anyone else. This perception however has a private meaning for him, and the second state, which is the development of the delusion, follows almost immediately. The crystallisation of an elaborate delusional system following upon the percept is often very sudden. The delusional perception is frequently preceded by a delusional atmosphere.'[151]

Commonly, of course, multiple symptoms are present, and the patient describes a gamut of experiences, as did Andrew, a simple man, when he said, 'There are robots, one left and one right; Queen Elizabeth on top [of my head] rules them all . . . visions going through my head from a space station'.

There has been wide agreement that these symptoms are characteristic of schizophrenia. In Mellor's 1970 study of patients diagnosed as schizophrenic on admission to an English mental hospital, 72 per cent had first-rank symptoms, and 'a majority of the patients diagnosed as schizophrenic, but without first-rank symptoms on mental examination, had typical schizophrenic defect states [i.e. had been left disabled by the aftermath of the acute illness]. In 12 of these cases there was adequate documentary evidence for inferring that they had experienced first-rank symptoms in the past.'[151] In total, at least 79 per cent of the patients were known to have had these characteristic symptoms.

Schneider stated that it is very hard to discern a common factor in these experiences. However, some – the feelings of thought-withdrawal, thought-influence, thought-broadcasting and being influenced and manipulated in general – can be considered to be expressive of a disorder of the perception of the boundary between the self and the outside world.

Normally we have an approximate understanding of this mysterious matter, certainly enough of a working comprehension to live with. We assume that our body and personality end, in a sense, at the finger-tips, although it is insufficient to say that. Our clothes may become almost part of our personality, and we certainly express ourselves in complicated styles beyond our finger-tips when playing the piano or driving a car. We will also agree that, in another sense, the body is inessential to some aspects of the personality, and only the mind counts as the essential self. Amputation of a limb is scarcely felt to truncate the personality.

In general, we can move our limbs by our familiar but utterly mysterious willpower, and our thoughts are our own, in our minds. Assuming that telepathy and psychokinesis do not occur to any significant extent, we know that we cannot move other people's limbs by the same willpower, and they cannot move ours except by applying force from outside. We cannot read or influence their thoughts directly, nor can they ours. There is a boundary between the self with its inner world and the environment in the outer world, and the boundary is clear.

In the schizophrenic experiences, the line of the boundary is blurred and pervious: inner and outer worlds do not feel safely distinct. Hence the feelings that thoughts are influenced from outside and in their turn may broadcast outwards to the world. The experience is frightening and disruptive, and the associated explanatory delusions (that it is caused by a black magic device operated by an unseen enemy, for example) provide explanations and bring partial order out of chaos.

Privacy is no longer inviolate: one of Kraepelin's patients said: 'When I leave the house all the telephones know where I am going and what I am thinking.'[106] Laing puts it as follows:

If [the person] feels not only that his own privacy is lost to him, but also that he is granted access to the privacy of others, his life will be no less tormented. It is common to find that such a person is as tormented by his feeling that he can read other people's minds and discover their secrets, as he is by his sense of his own lack of privacy. . . . The loss of the experience of *unqualified privacy* of this area [one's own self-being], by its transformation into a quasi-public realm, is often one of the decisive changes associated with the process of going mad.[109]

The suggestion that schizophrenic experiences can be seen in this way recalls the interest shown by some patients, during the premonitory phases of their illness, in pursuits on this very borderland between the self and the outside world, concerning influence at a distance, occult manipulation and the power of the mind. They study hypnosis, dabble in black magic, believe in telepathy, take up spiritualism or practise with the ouija board.

Schneider argued that this explanation in terms of a perviousness of the boundary between the mind and the outside world does not apply, without forcing the facts, to the hallucinatory experiences and the delusional perception of being 'made' to feel and act. Surely he is wrong here, for these experiences do indeed indicate disturbance of the boundary, so that thoughts are confused with voices perceived from the outside world, and there is a loss of the normal assumption and feeling that only the self in the inner world of the mind is the mediator of emotions and initiator of willed actions. All hallucinations, whether in mental illness or in health (in states of exhaustion, sensory deprivation, and when drifting off to sleep), indicate disturbance in this area, and it is particularly marked in schizophrenia.

Emotional disorder

Profound emotional disturbance is a typical part of schizophrenia, although it can take many different forms. Traditional psychiatry recognised *emotional incongruity*, referring, for example, to patients who giggle or laugh outright 'incongruously' in inappropriate situations. However, this has proved vulnerable to the criticism that the incongruity is in the judgment of the psychiatrist, in his world, his culture, his class, leading his life, and from his god-like position. Perhaps psychiatrists are humourless, or at least are insensitive to satire, irony, sick and black humour. Who knows but that the schizophrenic may have excellent reasons for roaring with laughter at his mother's demise, if the theories about schizophrenogenic mothers contain even a little truth? Perhaps it can be more appropriate to laugh than to cry at many of the peculiar incidents occurring in psychiatric wards. The solitary, deteriorated patient in the back ward of the mental hospital, silent all day except when he chuckles and guffaws with laughter about jokes that he never reveals, is doubtless laughing at *something,* and we have an uneasy feeling that he may have good reason. Emotional incongruity as a confidently diagnosed sign has become obsolete after Laing's criticism[113] of the lordly insensitivity of psychiatrists' categorisation of tormented patients.

The same considerations apply to *emotional flattening.* The psychiatrist must be very sure of his own criteria and their applicability to the patient, before attributing emotional unreactivity to him when the patient is apparently unmoved by striking events around him, even by those that affect him personally. There could be much misclassification of Stoics by Epicureans, and of Northern (allegedly dour, stiff upper-lip) by Southern (over-emotional) Europeans.

Yet flattening of emotional reactivity certainly describes an aspect of schizophrenia as seen by people around the patient. His family or workmates describe the change from his former self to his colourless present condition, and the end-state of impassivity in response to the environment, as seen in the chronic patient, is real enough. In the International Pilot Study of Schizophrenia, described more fully in Chapter 4, schizophrenic patients had high scores for flatness of affect in all nine centres studied, and in the core group of schizophrenics picked by agreement between clinical diagnosis and statistical and computer methods, 65 per cent of the patients were described as showing this feature.

Many other emotional disturbances may occur to a severe degree in schizophrenia, while not themsleves being infallible signs of the condition. I have already discussed the moods in which all events seem invested with the greatest significance. The atmosphere is often one of terrifying menace. The mood may be one of the greatest bewilderment about what is felt to be happening around the patient and what he feels is being done to him, as he tries to grasp the meaning of it all: a typical state which is described externally and clinically in psychiatric textbooks, and internally and sympathetically in *The divided self.*[110]

Depression may be the obvious affective change for long periods, and may, especially in adolescence, usher in the whole schizophrenic process, masking more characteristic symptoms. Periods of great excitement and of violent anger also occur, sometimes erupting suddenly and with little external provocation.

Disorders of activity and movement

In schizophrenia, there are manifold disorders of general activity, disturbances of instinctual drive, especially of sexual behaviour, and distortions of bodily movement known as catatonia. Again, our descriptions are outward and clinical in comparison with the flights of empathic understanding to be found in Laing's books and to be gleaned direct from the patients by those willing to listen and wait to be trusted.

The withdrawal of interest and absorption from the outer world into the inner one – the *autism* of E. Bleuler[14] – is reflected in inactivity. The patient may sit motionless for hours staring into space, night and day. Among the scurrying crowds on the pavement, he suddenly stands stock-still, listening, turning around as he hearkens to his inner voices, oblivious to passers-by who must walk round him. At home, he hardly leaves his room, shows little inclination to get out of bed, and never washes himself or his clothes. Rubbish may collect and be ignored, so that neglected schizophrenic patients are some-times found, as was Mr A. R., in airless, stinking bed-sitting rooms piled high with junk, old newspapers, empty tins of food, torn books and old letters, with the patient himself wearing grimy clothes that have been unchanged for months.

He may be as oblivious to heat, cold and discomfort as he is to public opinion, becoming known as the local madman by his utterly inappropriate dress in the street – half naked in the cold, or with layers of ancient jerseys and overcoats in the heat, but in any case eccentric at all times.

Sexual behaviour may be utterly disrupted, too, psychiatrists referring to typical *chaotic sexuality*. The withdrawal from the conventional constraints of the social world, and the alienation from being bound by it, result in many complaints from those around the patient. Homosexual experiments and fetishistic forays may occur in previously heterosexual individuals. Most commonly, the patients masturbate openly or more frequently, and apparently blithely, on inappropriate occasions. Schizophrenic sons may display sexual interest in their mothers when they masturbate, or may offer to share their bed.

The catatonic disorders affect the action of the body, its posture and the style of its movements. The muscles are not paralysed or weakened, nor are the powers of coordination lost as they are in diseases of the brain. However, movements can be used as expressions of the personality and for communication, and in the schizophrenic with catatonic disorder, the disturbed relationship of the person with the world seems to be expressed in the body as well as in speech and the other ways already described.

Much of this behaviour is an expression of extreme withdrawal of action, as well as interest and emotion, from the outside world. Some patients never speak, although they understand all that is said to them. They may recover rapidly, but some handicapped schizophrenics in the wards of mental hospitals used to go for decades without uttering a single word. Sometimes the expression on the face of the patient looks blank, but more often it suggests an intense preoccupation with bewildering thoughts, which is often confirmed by the patient after he recovers.

These intensely withdrawn patients usually move very slowly or scarcely at all – until the last 20 years, some hospital wards contained patients who stood for long periods like statues, often in awkward positions, and with expressionless faces. A typical feature of catatonic patients, taught without fail to generations of psychiatrists in training, is the way their limbs can be moved around by the examiner as if they belonged to a wire model. Limbs left in unsupported positions remain there for a time before slowly drooping with gravity (so-called 'waxy flexibility'); similarly, the head of the patient may stay in the air after his pillow has been removed (the 'psychological pillow').

Even the superficial observer can soon notice, however, that there is more to it than such a negative, if intriguing, description. There are resistances and negativisms, sometimes during the manipulation, sometimes afterwards when the examiner is not looking. The patient is turned away from the doctor more than just accidentally, and is unhelpful to him. When he follows the doctor's actions and echoes his speech ('echolalia' and 'echopraxia'), could he be teasing and mimicking him?

Kraepelin and Laing

The dawning suspicion of sensitive psychiatrists that the awkwardness they sometimes felt with these patients was induced by the patients' alienation, hauteur or even hostility and contempt was confirmed in

Laing's famous re-interpretation of an interview by Kraepelin, to be found at the beginning of *The divided self*.[113] Kraepelin, respected founding-father of descriptive clinical psychiatry, had defined dementia praecox, the term which was a precursor of schizophrenia, and his textbook ran to nine editions.[105] Many psychiatric textbooks open their chapters on schizophrenia with a passage on Kraepelin.

In 1905, he was examining a patient and demonstrating catatonic excitement, in which the slowed, withdrawn patient becomes wildly overactive and disordered in speech and action. The patient behaved oddly and unpredictably, with a peculiar walk, singing loudly and then shutting his eyes. His talk, angry, irritated, off the point at a tangent and expressed in peculiar sentences, was described by Kraepelin as 'only a series of disconnected sentences having no relation whatever to the general situation'. Laing has no difficulty in showing convincingly that there was indeed a relation to the general situation, Kraepelin and his followers being made to seem insensitive, and deaf to subtleties (although they too have an important point of view, that of descriptive scientific psychiatry). Laing says of the patient, 'Surely he is carrying on a dialogue between his own parodied version of Kraepelin, and his own defiant self . . . presumably he deeply resents this form of interrogation . . . Now it seems clear that this patient's behaviour can be seen in at least two ways . . . one may see his behaviour as "signs" of a "disease"; one may see his behaviour as expressive of his existence.'[113]

The course of the condition

The course of the illness and disablement is very varied, and depends to an important extent on the breadth of the original definition of cases as being truly schizophrenic. Transient states of undoubted mental illness with fleeting delusions and hallucinations for a few hours at a time of great emotional turmoil are quite common, clear up rapidly, and are not called schizophrenic. The concept of schizophrenia, since its beginnings with Kraepelin[105] and E. Bleuler,[14] was always intended to embrace the severely 'ill', disturbed people – originally Kraepelin's inpatients at Munich, and those of Bleuler in the Burghölzli cantonal mental hospital in Zürich. The condition of the typical patient was thought to deteriorate irreversibly, at least to some extent, leaving disability of personality; few patients given the diagnostic label recovering completely.

Research on schizophrenia has been bedevilled by the failure to agree, especially internationally, on whether it is to be diagnosed on the basis of common disorders such as delusions or hallucinations (in which case some patients have acute brief illnesses and recover), or whether the label should be withheld except in the presence of a cluster of 'nuclear', characteristic, longer lasting features (when it is found that the patients go on to suffer much more severe disablement with very few recoveries). Psychiatrists have not always been as clear as they should have been that if they wait for the signs of ingrained disablement before diagnosing the illness, then it is by definition rather than by observation an incurable condition.

Recent international research, described in the next chapter, has shown much agreement about the main features of the condition, and it is certain that many different courses occur, even after typical early symptoms. Acutely disturbed patients may recover completely, never to be mentally ill again. Yet the same syndrome in other patients may be followed by relapse at any interval from days to decades, and in the intervals there may be greater or lesser degrees of deterioration. In general, each episode increases the danger of irreversible damage to the personality. Mr T. I. recovered and pursued a responsible, professional career without impairment of his former self; Mrs B. D. never recovered fully after her second illness, and was left strange, remote with other people, and possessed of abnormal thoughts about what it had all meant.

We know about the fate of schizophrenics diagnosed on admission to hospital earlier in this century from the remarkable Swiss research of Manfred Bleuler, son of Eugen Bleuler who had named the condition, and from the work of Ciompi. M. Bleuler has painstakingly traced the progress of the 212 schizophrenics admitted to the Burghölzli Hospital in 1942–3, for over 20 years to 1964–5.[15] In the 1940s and early 1950s, the treatment would have consisted of a hospital, the regime including simple forms of sedation, diversion and occupation, and any activity thought to promote strengthening and healing of the healthy part of the personality. Most of the 20 years studied fell before the introduction of the more specific drug teatment for schizophrenia in 1953. M. Bleuler seems anyway not to have been enthusiastic about the advantages of the new drug treatments of the last three decades.

He says that he saw nearly all the patients admitted from the canton, and that those admitted from the same area to a variety of private hospitals were similar in type and severity to his own patients. We are assured that he used relatively narrow diagnostic criteria – the diagnosis depended on a severely abnormal mental state at the time. He lost touch with only four of the patients, remaining in contact with 208. These certainly included a wide spectrum of patients, aged from 16 to 67, and, of the total, 66 (32 per cent) were experiencing their first admission to a psychiatric hospital. Over 20 years later, 70 of the patients had died – 12 during treatment for the acute illness (none of these 12 would be expected to die nowadays) and nine by suicide (which is a risk in schizophrenia, although much less so than in severe depression). He found that a half to three-quarters of the patients reached a long-lasting steady state after 10 years; a quarter to a third were apparently cured; one-tenth to a fifth were in a state of severe chronic psychosis; and the remainder were in a mild psychotic state.

Ciompi[26] traced surviving patients in their old age, on average 37 years after their first admission to mental hospital. A quarter of them had become asylum patients, each staying inside for over 20 years but, on the other hand, a half had been in hospital for altogether less than a single year of their lives. Half of all the patients had done very well (27 per cent having recovered completely and 22 per cent being left with slight changes in their personality or social adjustment) and most of the other half had deteriorated mentally.

Pritchard[166] made a more recent study of the prognosis of schizophrenia, in particular before and after the introduction of the drugs which are now a mainstay of the standard regimes of treatment all over the world. He studied the fate of 50 patients admitted to the academic unit at the Maudsley Hospital in London in 1952–3 and of 50 patients admitted there in 1956–7. The unit concentrated on short-term treatment for selected cases, so the patients under study were a selected group, and all were in hospital voluntarily. The study excluded the more severely disturbed. In 1952 and 1953, there were some early methods of physical treatment in use, including the induction of insulin coma (which was subsequently shown to have no specific effect). In 1956 and 1957, the new phenothiazine drugs had been introduced in the form of chlorpromazine (Largactil), which many of the patients received.

In the short term, up to a year after admission, the patients in the later group, most of whom had been treated with the new drug, had fared considerably better than the earlier ones in terms of the factor that could be counted in this retrospective study, namely length of stay in hospital. Thirteen of the earlier group of 50 had had to be transferred from the Maudsley Hospital to mental hospitals elsewhere, in the expectation of a long spell in hospital or of the need for detention, while only two of the later 50 had been transferred. The length of stay in the Maudsley Hospital, or in the Maudsley Hospital plus the mental hospital, was much longer in the earlier period than in the later.

It has been suggested that improvements in morale and the introduction of an open style in psychiatric hospitals may have contributed to or even have been the main cause of the apparent improvement in the prospects for schizophrenics since the 1950s. However, in the case of the academic unit, it is probable that there had been no significant general improvement in conditions in the 4-year interval between 1952 and 1956. Thus, Pritchard concludes that: 'Pharmacotherapy has resulted in an improved short-term prognosis in schizophrenia.' He thought that this was especially true of the patients who had been thought on admission to have poor prospects, whereas the patients with a better chance of recovery seemed to do equally well with the older and newer forms of treatment. We shall find this theme again in a later study of drug treatment (see Ch. 10[129]). As nearly all schizophrenic patients are given specific treatment nowadays, the present prognosis may well be better than in these older long-term studies.

4

Other places

In Chapter 2, I described some of the thousands of patients who are undoubtedly schizophrenic. However, there are problems in defining this illness, and it is important that the same definition is used by different research studies when their results are to be compared.

How many people with strange forms of thinking and behaviour should be diagnosed as schizophrenic, as opposed to being regarded as depressed, suffering from other mental illness, or as eccentric, idiosyncratic or even holy? Are psychiatrists at different times and places consistent in their diagnosis of schizophrenia, or indeed are they consistent when they share the same time and place? Furthermore, does schizophrenia occur in other parts of the world where cultures are very different from our own, and did it occur in remote eras of past history? If so, does it differ in form, modified by the culture in which it has developed?

In the last chapter, I said that there was general agreement that a diagnosis of schizophrenia could be made in a patient experiencing the highly characteristic symptoms described by Schneider. However, these symptoms are found clearly in only some of the patients, and therefore the diagnosis is usually made on the basis of the whole syndrome, including phenomena such as hallucinations that by themselves are not unique to schizophrenia. A requirement of unusual symptoms for the diagnosis of schizophrenia would make it a rarer disease; inclusion of more common ones makes it commoner. The rarer disease with so-called 'nuclear' symptoms has a poor prognosis, the patients tending to deteriorate into severely handicapped states, while lax diagnostic criteria can result in the inclusion of the mildly ill whose condition borders on mere eccentricity, and many of these do well, returning to their former, albeit sometimes odd, selves.

Psychiatrists had long suspected from working on both sides of the Atlantic, and from textbook descriptions, that schizophrenia was more readily diagnosed in parts of the USA than in the United Kingdom, and in fact sometimes in America cases were included that would be described in the UK as depressed, manic or as life-long 'schizoid' aloof personalities. This belief was investigated by Cooper *et al.* in their study entitled *Psychiatric diagnosis in New York and London,*[37] which confirmed that a difference in diagnostic habits did indeed exist. All patients in the study who were diagnosed as schizophrenic in London were similarly diagnosed in New York, but other patients, given different diagnoses in London, were called schizophrenic in New York, because a wider definition of the illness is taught there. Generalisation farther afield is not possible: for example, the diagnostic pattern in St Louis has been found to be rather different again. The research confirmed the existence of typical schizophrenics in both centres, and showed the need for caution in comparing such figures as the frequency of schizophrenia in particular countries.

The demonstration of typical patients on both sides of the Atlantic is a modest achievement, however. It would be more important to discover if typical schizophrenia occurs in more diverse cultures.

Much progress has been made in cross-cultural studies of diagnosis by the International Pilot Study of Schizophrenia (IPSS).[240] In this remarkable work, psychiatrists co-operated in similar methods of examination and diagnosis of comparable patients in nine different centres in widely different social settings. The centres were: Aarhus, Denmark; Agra, India; Cali, Colombia; Ibadan, Nigeria; London, England; Moscow, Russia; Prague, Czechoslovakia; Taipei, Taiwan; and Washington, DC, USA. Unfortunately, no centre in Germany was included despite the prominent part played by this country in the development of psychiatric thinking. In addition, the omission of a French centre meant the loss of an opportunity to help reduce the isolation of French psychiatry from that of most of the rest of the world. The aim of the study was to answer the questions: 'In what sense can it be said that schizophrenic disorders exist in different parts of the world? Do they differ in form and content? Does the clinical course differ?'

In their introduction, the researchers outline the most usual view among psychiatrists on schizophrenia and 'cultural relativism', that is that schizophrenia certainly occurs in widely different cultures, although probably at different rates. They state that the factors favouring schizophrenia as the subject for the first study were that

there was [i.e. already before the study started] a certain degree of agreement as to the chief features of at least a central group of disorders given this label; that numerous surveys had already been made and approximate incidence and prevalence rates established; that there was some evidence that the condition occurred at approximately the same rate in populations differing as widely as those of Bavaria, Bornholm, Baltimore, Taiwan, Japan, London and Moscow; that almost the whole spectrum of psychopathology of the functional [i.e. not ordinary brain disease] psychiatric disorders would be covered; and that the degree of severity and chronicity was such that in all societies schizophrenia was a personally crippling and socially damaging disease. In addition there was an element of uncertainty to investigate, since some studies had shown very high rates or very low rates of schizophrenia in isolated populations. Although the disease concept of schizophrenia had been challenged, no author had been able to produce an array of evidence in favour of any other approach, or to show that an alternative concept would lead to a more useful way of studying what everyone agreed was a recognizable behavioural syndrome.[240]

The method was to study a group of similar patients in every centre. The patients were all aged between 15 and 44 years, with onset of illness within the previous 5 years. Those selected had not had severe mental illness for more than 3 years, because it was thought that chronicity might obscure the clarity of symptoms.

Patients were excluded from the study if they had been inpatients for more than 2 years of the previous 5, since they might have exhibited symptoms not unique to schizophrenia but caused by chronic hospitalisation, and if they regularly abused alcohol or drugs that affect the brain, to avoid confusion with states of physical illness caused by ordinary poisoning of cerebral processes. Those with other physical illnesses of or affecting the brain, such as epilepsy, were also excluded as were those patients grossly handicapped in intelligence. Finally, the study also excluded patients with difficulties of communication that would have greatly impeded interviewing, such as severe deafness, severe stammering or very unusual dialects. Such cases having been omitted from consideration, 100 consecutive patients with severe mental illness who contacted the local psychiatric service were examined with a standard interview schedule, the Present State Examination. This has been shown to give reliable and repeatable results in the hands of psychiatrists trained in its use.

It was found that similar profiles of symptoms were used in all the centres for some patients diagnosed as schizophrenic, and 'similar groups of schizophrenics can be identified in every one of the nine countries'. In all the centres, the patients commonly agreed to be schizophrenic typically lacked insight into the fact that their behaviour was abnormal, and experienced phenomena commonly leading to delusions (such as an intense feeling that everything was pregnant with meaning, ideas that everything around them seemed especially to refer to them, and feelings of perplexity about what was going on). They showed flattening of the normal person's fluctuations in depth of feeling, suffered experiences of being controlled by mysterious influences, and had auditory hallucinations (which symptom was, however, not so typical of the patients in Washington). In general, these findings must be seen as a vindication of the view that schizophrenia occurs in a typical form in at least some cases in widely differing cultures, although this is certainly not to say that the syndrome is not more common in some places than in others, nor that the natural course of the condition does not vary considerably under different conditions.

The research, therefore, showed that typical cases of severe schizophrenia, as described in textbooks of psychiatry, and centring on delusions, hallucinations, flattening of affect and lack of insight, occur in the nine places studied. In addition, the boundaries set for the syndrome, illustrated by the types of cases that were excluded by the psychiatrists and by their computer-assisted diagnostic process as *not* schizophrenic, were remarkably similar in seven of the nine centres. The diagnosis of schizophrenia was, in fact, very similar in Aarhus, Agra, Cali, Ibadan, London, Taipei and Prague. In Washington and Moscow, on the other hand, the diagnostic process was rather different, and this was because in these centres there was a notably wider and different concept of schizophrenia.

In Washington, the broad definition included eccentric personalities with difficulties in their relationships, and also patients whose severe mental illness with its prime features of elation and overactivity would have been diagnosed in most other centres as a different condition, namely mania. The differences in diagnostic practice between much of the United States and Europe have long been realised, and have their principal explanation in the history of the development of psychiatry in the USA. The psychoanalytical movement took firm root there, and psychodynamic concepts came to dominate psychiatric education and practice. This in turn affected diagnostic habits, with a blurring of the boundaries of differing psychiatric conditions. Psychoanalysis has never been a stimulus for scientific research, or for the description and classification of syndromes.

Thus, schizophrenia came to be construed in the USA in terms of a disturbed relationship of the personality with the world, while in Europe 'descriptive' and 'phenomenological' psychiatry concentrated, when trying to clarify the problems of diagnosis, on the form of the symptoms themselves, as I have done in Chapter 3.

In Moscow, the unusually wide definition of schizophrenia depended on a lesser emphasis on the mental symptoms of the patient and more on detailed considerations of the course of his life, and changes in his degree of adjustment to society. The influential teaching of Snezhnevsky[207,234] describes these different courses, which can be for example: 'periodic', with episodes of disorder followed by complete recovery; 'shift', when each acute episode is followed by only partial recovery and some permanent deterioration; or 'sluggish' with slow insidious deterioration of adjustment. Mental state is specified somewhat vaguely.

This state of affairs has contributed to the difficulty of Western psychiatrists in unequivocally condemning the Russian practice of confining political dissidents in forensic mental hospitals on the grounds of schizophrenia manifest as change of personality and 'reformist delusions'. The defenders of the system can point to the broad definition of schizophrenia, including 'delusions of reconstruction or reformation', sincerely expressed in textbooks, which throws up a smokescreen around the cynical exploitation of psychiatry for the hidden suppression of political dissent.

Let it be quite clearly understood that there is no similarity between the incarceration of notable intellectuals in Soviet mental hospitals, and the fact that England, like other countries, has a secure hospital for the few mentally ill patients who are truly dangerous. Broadmoor Hospital houses only severely and dangerously disturbed patients; there are no politically disaffected intellectuals there.

As for China, little has been published in the West about the concept of schizophrenia there. One piece of information suggests that schizophrenia certainly exists at an unsurprising frequency, so that it cannot possibly be a result of alienation from late-capitalist society and the domination of the military–industrial complex. A senior psychiatrist in Shanghai is quoted by Kety[102] as saying that, in China, 'We think the incidence is the same [i.e. as in the West]. But our communities accept the patients more readily and we treat them there. We rely heavily on outpatient services and on phenothiazine drugs, but we do a lot of education of the patient's family and his co-workers so that our patients can be released from the hospital and be accepted by the community.' Another report describes high rates of schizophrenia.[141]

Educational notices in the Shanghai Psychiatric Institute include among the symptoms of psychosis: '. . . hearing voices that criticise, abuse, threaten them or give them orders, or that they see strange things, smell strange smells. Some are full of suspicion and feel persecuted . . . some are still as statues, they neither eat nor drink and are unable to relieve themselves. All these clinical symptoms distinguish them from normal persons.'[22]

In India, as we have seen, the IPSS found typical schizophrenics, as described in European textbooks, in Agra. There have been some studies on the frequency of the condition, and on its prognosis, to ascertain whether the condition is indeed different in different places. Elnagar,[49] in a thorough house-to-house survey of a village in rural India, found six cases of schizophrenia which had started when the victims were between the ages of 6 and 40 years. This was in a village of 1383 people, so the condition was not rare. European studies have usually found rates of around 8 per 1000 – not very much higher.

A study of the chronicity of schizophrenia in a mainly urban area around Chandigarh, north-west India, was carried out by Kulhara and Wig,[108] and the results were compared with those of a survey in London by Brown et al.[21] who used similar methods. In both studies, schizophrenia was diagnosed using the 'First-rank symptoms' of Schneider, which are the usual criteria of British psychiatrists, and which are described in the previous chapter. Kulhara and Wig recorded clear-cut cases amongst adults and tried to trace these patients 5 years later. Only two-thirds of the patients originally studied could be found. Thirty-two per cent of these were chronically disturbed, 23 per cent were disturbed by episodes of schizophrenia from time to time, 16 per cent were improving and although odd were not psychotic (i.e. not mentally ill), and 29 per cent were no longer disturbed. These figures are remarkably similar to those of Brown et al., who found in their London study, 28, 27, 11 and 34 per cent, respectively, in the same categories. The Indian authors commented that the similarity of outcome implied a benign course of the illness in India, because in comparison with London there was only a rudimentary psychiatric service, poor aftercare, and very little treatment with drugs. Despite these disadvantages the patients fared comparably with those studied in England. Kulhara and Wig thought that there was a high degree of acceptance of disturbed behaviour by the patients' families.

Another study from Asia was that of Murphy and Raman[153,167] in Mauritius, where conditons on the island with only one mental hospital were favourable for studying the frequency of the illness and keeping in touch with patients over long periods. Admission rates to hospital, widely used as a rough measure of the frequency of schizophrenia, on the assumption that a high proportion of cases are admitted at some time during the course of the illness, were similar to those in England. The patients were treated by traditional forms of nursing care rather than with modern drugs, and 60 per cent of them were leading normal lives with no history of relapse when traced 12 years after their admission. Brown et al. in England, and authors of other studies on European and American populations in the 1950s and early 1960s, found only 30–50 per cent of the patients doing well a few years later.[15,20,26]

Murphy and Raman conclude that, in this mainly poor Indo-African population, there is a better overall prognosis than in London. In particular, they thought that mild forms of schizophrenia had a better prognosis than in England, but that in the more severe cases 'the proportions remaining severely disabled (at long-term follow-up) are virtually the same'.[153]

Neki,[155] in a review of this subject in India, maintains that the pattern of schizophrenic illness varies in different cultures. He quotes high rates in that country for the catatonic type of illness, which he is inclined to attribute to a delay in consultation until the disease has run a severe course without medical intervention. He found 'simple' schizophrenia, the type with predominantly slow and insidious chronic symptoms, to be rare in India. Patients with this form of the illness tend to become apathetic and uninterested in practical activity. Their thinking becomes vague and abstract, and fine feelings for family and conventions are lost. Such patients give up work, cease any fruitful activity, may no longer wash, sometimes stay in bed, and may enter an inactive almost immobile state resembling a trance. Sometimes they continue to converse with those around them, although usually not spontaneously, on abstract topics imprecisely expressed (the 'pseudophilosophical ideas' of psychiatric description). The state is a disability and cause for grave concern to the patient's family when it occurs in England – innumerable rules are broken to the despair of all around. However, Neki says that in India, where these people are scattered in the pastoral community, they are tolerated, and may even be honoured as religious mendicants, a role not open to them in less religious industrial countries.

Around the world, follow-up of the IPSS patients[241] is confirming that schizophrenia has a better prognosis in developing countries than in Europe and America.

In Africa, there have been a number of studies of mental illness in the native peoples, mostly by European psychiatrists, and the results have been reviewed by German.[62] There is agreement that acute transient psychoses, with violently disturbed behaviour, are common among illiterate Africans, and they can be seen to be precipitated very often by obvious personal upsets. Some of these psychoses are, in fact, forms of delirium caused by cerebral dysfunction and clouding of consciousness in the course of physical illness, for example with high fever. Delusions and hallucinations may be suspected by observers and sometimes are certainly present, so that it can be difficult to decide whether these conditions should be classified as schizophrenia. If they are, the general prognosis of schizophrenia improves since many of these cases recover completely. Similar psychoses occurred in Europe in earlier times, giving rise to the same dilemma concerning diagnosis, but are now less common among the native-born. However, some of the West Indian population in England are liable to brief but very disturbed psychoses that resemble schizophrenia in all aspects except their tendency to rapid and complete recovery. These acute illnesses are not at all typical of the long-lasting condition that has been understood by the term schizophrenia, ever since it was coined by Bleuler,[14] who expanded and revised Kraepelin's concept of dementia praecox.[105]

Whether or not these acute psychoses should be defined as schizophrenia, there are reports from Africa of cases of schizophrenia of a more chronic type as found in classical European descriptions. The IPSS found cases in Nigeria, and German noted that chronic schizophrenia occurs in all classes of Africans, and that, for example, in the mental hospital in Kampala in Uganda most of the chronic patients are schizophrenics of all types.[62]

Is the case proven that schizophrenia occurs in all cultures? The psychiatrists of the IPSS certainly found it in nine varied cultures. Yet two other possibilities still remain. One is that they found schizophrenia because as psychiatrists they tended to label and diagnose people as mentally ill who were merely awkward and eccentric, deviant and dissenting. I shall return to this theme in Chapter 8. Another possibility is that the nine cultures studied by the IPSS were not fully representative as they were all relatively advanced. They all had, for example, a psychiatric service of some sort that was sufficiently sophisticated to allow research. Truly backward cultures might be different. I shall therefore look at some studies of mental illness in remote cultures.

From Central Australia, Cawte and Kidson[24, 25] described mental illness among the aboriginal Walbiri people, who live in a remote area north-west of Alice Springs. This tribe had hardly any contact with white people until after the end of World War 2, but in the 1960s became economically dependent on government rations.

An account of the illness of Darkie Tjapaltjari goes as follows:

This elderly man has a history of psychoses in middle life, but in earlier days he was a famous and respected doctor. Even sophisticated part-aboriginal cattlemen had great faith in his diagnostic and curative powers. However, fifteen years ago, *wangamara* (madness) came on. Darkie had left Mt. Doreen to live at Haast Bluff when his young wife died. He acted strangely, was seclusive and became violent if people approached. He joined tin cans to lengths of wire, saying it was his wireless and forbidding people to talk near it. He chopped up tin lids with an axe in the belief that he was making money. It was surmised that some evil-wisher had 'sung' (enchanted) his tobacco.

After people started calling him *wangamara* and Mad Darkie, he retired from practice as a doctor. He now carries out the simple task of sweeping an area of ground outside one of the settlement buildings and seems proud of his efforts. He flies into rages, but is easily distracted from them by being given a book. He will chatter with any white person without comprehending the conversation. His buffoon-like mimicry of white ways still earns him the name Mad Darkie, and he needs to be sedated for other people's comfort because of his temper.[25]

Darkie is evidently a schizophrenic of the type described in Europe. The history of his illness spans 15 years and he has survived without medical treatment of the original illness, so the diagnosis cannot be a cerebral condition such as a brain tumour or late syphilis. He went insane, with bizarre behaviour and probably delusions, and was left in a deteriorated state. In his illness, he even mocks the sane world around him from the unassailable position of the madman, as Laing has pointed out that his patients were doing.[110] Yet there is a tantalising glimpse of psychiatric intervention: the patient is being sedated (surely by the white man) 'for other people's comfort'.

Another case from the same tribe, Kitty Naparula, was regarded as normal until she became adult, when she

had several self-limiting episodes of severe mental disturbance, in nearly every instance associated with childbirth. Eight years ago whilst pregnant she complained of noises in the ear, and talked to herself in a way that could not be understood. She appeared frightened and vague. This *wangamara* brought her teasing from camp-fellows, who are customarily amused by sickness or emotional instability. She reacted with violence and excitement, and the Flying Doctor recommended transfer to Alice Springs Hospital late in 1956. In 1957 she was vague and obstinate and was again sent to Alice Springs Hospital for mental illness but after 2 months absconded and walked home. In 1958 she gave birth to Jonathan (who subsequently died) and there was another episode of irresponsibility and excitement. In 1960 she was again agitated but responded to Largactil. In 1963, again pregnant, she became disturbed, shouting at society in general and threatening with a club. After the birth of the baby in the camp she was miserable and could not breast-feed the child; in pre-settlement days it would not have survived.[25]

This story is not very different from that of some European patients. The noises in the ears and the talking to herself indicate vivid auditory hallucinations, and, together with the period of vagueness, suggest that she suffered from recurrent schizophrenic illness, although another possible diagnosis would be recurrent mania, or perhaps an intermediate type of illness. Note that the madness was laughed at by her fellows, and the medical intervention was a humanitarian one, to prevent further cruelty to her in her own environment, and to forestall her reaction to the cruelty.

Murphy,[154] an anthropologist, studied mental illness in two exotic cultures, the Eskimos of north-west Alaska and the Yorubas of rural Nigeria. She records that she had expected to confirm a cultural relativist position in which there would be no universals of madness or schizophrenia, and in which every culture would create and label its own varieties of unacceptable behaviour. However, she was forced to conclude from her research that there were common patterns of disturbance everywhere, recognised as mental illness by the local people.

Among the Eskimos, *nuthkavihak,* translated by them into English as 'being crazy', was manifested by

talking to oneself, screaming at someone who does not exist, believing that a child or husband was murdered by witchcraft when nobody else believes it, believing oneself to be an animal, refusing to eat for fear eating will kill one, refusing to talk, running away, getting lost, hiding in strange places, making strange grimaces, drinking urine, becoming strong and violent, killing dogs, and threatening people. . . . There is a Yoruba word *were,* which is also translated as insanity. The phenomena include hearing voices and trying to get other people to see their source though none can be seen, laughing when there is nothing to laugh at, talking all the time or not talking at all, asking oneself questions and answering them, picking up sticks and leaves for no purpose except to put them in a pile, throwing away food because it is thought to contain *juju,* tearing off one's clothes, setting fires, defaecating in public and then mushing around in the faeces, taking up a weapon and suddenly hitting someone with it, breaking things in a state of being stronger than normal, believing that an odor is continuously being emitted from one's body.

Murphy found that for both *nuthkavihak* and *were* indigenous healing practices were used, and, in fact, among the Yorubas some healers specialised in the treatment of *were*. The descriptions were never applied to a single symptom, such as hearing voices, but only to a pattern when several of the above phenomena existed together. The people of these tribes distinguished clearly between the syndromes of insanity and such phenomena as, for example, the ability to prophesy and to see things other people cannot: valued traits for diviners and shamans, who were far more common than the insane. One Eskimo said to Murphy: 'When the shaman is healing he is out of his mind, but *he is not crazy.*'

Murphy says, in a penetrating observation: 'This suggests that seeing, hearing and believing things that are not seen, heard and believed by all members of the group are sometimes linked to insanity and sometimes not. The distinction appears to be the degree to which they are controlled and utilized for a specific social function. The inability to control these processes is what is meant by a mind out of order: when a mind is out of order it not only fails to control sensory perception but will also fail to control behaviour.'

Field, studying the cases at rural healing shrines in Ashanti, Ghana, in the 1950s, was sure that schizophrenia occurred as the typical madness among those people, and she comments on the social adaptation of the victims in her very detailed study:

> If the stranger asks to be shown a madman he will probably be led to a florid schizophrenic. On the other hand, so long as a schizophrenic is accessible, talks coherently, is not destructive nor aggressive, and has only such delusions and hallucinations as are within the bounds of culturally determined credibility, he may fall a long way below social approval without being accounted mad. He may be thought idle, dirty, solitary, callous, heedless or perverse. In short if his friends say a man is *obodam* he is usually a schizophrenic, but he may be the latter, particularly of the simplex type, and 'get by'.[54]

She further says that the people understood the distinction between schizophrenia and the main other possible explanations of peculiar behaviour: epilepsy, mental handicap, trypanosomiasis (sleeping sickness) and 'spirit possession'.

She describes many cases. For example, a boy in his teens started wandering off into the bush, weeping and saying people were putting thoughts into his head. He said that people wanted to kill him, had made him blind and had broken all his bones. He ate only alone and continued to wander into the bush alone. He never washed or attended to himself.

A 17-year-old girl suddenly took off all her clothes and ran off into the bush. She was alternately violent and mutely inert. Sometimes the villagers locked her up to control her. She cried, sang, and talked to invisible people. When seen by Field she was mostly mute, vague and smiling inappropriately.[55]

A middle-aged woman was a quarrelsome, vigorously energetic person. She said that everyone was jealous because she had had so many lovers. She believed that enemies tampered with her drinking water, putting poison, ink and lime into it. She was not out of touch with the events of her life, but gave a disorganised story of stolen property and other grievances, with inappropriate smiling and giggling, and sometimes clapping and singing. 'People have taken all my land. One day when I was in the French Ivory Coast I was sitting down and a big lizard fell on me and someone gave me some kenkey to eat and that put something bad into my head, and now I have something like a heavy load on my head, and burnings like fire and something like a rope tied round my head.'[55]

In Nigeria, too, Murphy had found chronically disabled madmen: 'It was not uncommon to see *were* people wandering about the city streets, sometimes naked, more often dressed in odd assortments of tattered clothing, almost always with long dirt-laden hair, talking to themselves, picking up objects to save.'[154]

The stories from Ghana, and Murphy's brief description, are indistinguishable from those of many typical schizophrenics in London in the 1980s – and indeed anywhere else in the world where they are sought.

So, studies on the inhabitants of rural areas of Africa and Alaska, and on the most backward of people, the Australian aborigines, have found some cases with reasonably close similarities to European schizophrenics with regard to the main symptoms of the illness. It is clear that the illness arises everywhere, but the farther removed the culture is from that of Kraepelin and Bleuler in late 19th-century Europe, the less does the original syndrome resemble our tradition of schizophrenia. Not only does the content differ among the aborigines (spirit-fish and not microphones invade the body), but the form is not so regularly like that found in our patients: hallucinations occur, but elaborately systematised delusions may not.

Many psychiatrists maintain confidently that there is no problem of cultural relativity, because schizophrenia is an identifiable disease-entity that occurs in *all* cultures, just like measles or tuberculosis. Thus Dunham, renowned for research on culture and mental disorder, wrote in 1976: 'No social pyschological factor has been conclusively demonstrated to play a role in the development of schizophrenia;' 'Cultural relativism is of no value in explaining the psychosis;' 'The culture of a group can determine the content but not the forms of a psychosis;' and so 'Schizophrenia is found in every culture of the world.'[45] German,[62] states that the clinical picture of schizophrenia is the same in Africa as in Europe, and classical chronic schizophrenia occurs in all classes of African. Wittkower and Prince take the same line: 'There is now general agreement that schizophrenia is to be found in all cultures and that these clinical subforms [simple, hebephrenic, catatonic and paranoid] occur everywhere, though in varying frequencies. The alleged rarity of simple schizo-phrenia in some societies may be owing to the acceptance of low work performance by some communities.'[238] They add, as do most researchers, that the *content* of delusions and hallucinations is obviously moulded by culture.

Similarly, in a book on culture and mental disorders, Linton main-tains that, 'All the fundamental types of psychoses which are recognized by Europeans occur in other societies.'[140] Hence he believes that there must be an organic basis for the illness itself (in other words, a cerebral disturbance – a physical illness), with cultural determination of content.

The authors of the introductory chapter of the IPSS report wrote in the same vein, as I quoted early in this chapter, stating that there was 'some evidence' for the occurrence of schizophrenia at similar rates in widely different cultures. However, more modest than some authors, they did not insist that the illness has undoubtedly been found everywhere.

Yet the contrary view is no less persistently stated. Schizophrenia is ignored and only the concept of madness considered by authors like the French sociologist, Bastide,[7] who emphasises that madness depends wholly on the society in which the patient goes mad:

In the same way, anthropology shows that each society has its own 'correct way of going mad' and that this model is furnished by the myths or customs of the people . . . the sick person, to be recog-nized as sick, has to make his behaviour conform to the behaviour traditionally expected of the madman. Psychotics tend to develop the symptomatology that will enable the psychiatrist to classify their disturbances according to socially defined criteria. A Chippewa Indian tends to develop a *windigo* syndrome, a Malayan a *latah* psychosis. Fundamentally speaking, all madness is a form of *folie à deux* involving the psychiatrist and the patient, in which the psychiatrist represents the public (the collective conceptions of madness) and the patient endeavours to help him make his diag-nosis by taking the opposite course to the behaviour of normal people by making his disturbances into a ritual of rebellion.

This is similar to the position of Laing when he says, 'Sanity or psychosis is tested by the degree of conjunction or disjunction between two persons where the one is sane by common consent,'[113] and 'The "cause" of schizophrenia is to be found by the examination, not of the prospective diagnosee alone, but of the whole social context in which the psychiatric ceremonial is being conducted.'[120]

I have shown that there is strong evidence that this is wrong, for studies in the field in different cultures justify Murphy's conclusion:

It appears that (i) phenomenal processes of disturbed thought and behaviour similar to schizophrenia are found in most cultures; (ii) they are sufficiently distinctive and noticeable that almost everywhere a name has been created for them; (iii) over and above similarity in processes, there is variability in content which in a general way is coloured by culture; and (iv) the role of social fictions [i.e. labelling the disturbed people as suffering from a metaphorical mental illness] in perceiving and defining the phenomenon seems to have been very slight. . . . Patterns such as schizophrenia, *were* and *nuthkavihak* appear to be relatively rare in any one human group but are broadly distributed among human groups. Rather than being simply violations of the social norms of particular groups, symptoms of mental illness are manifestations of a type of affliction shared by virtually all mankind.[154]

5
Other times

One of the main themes of this book is whether a schizophrenic kind of insanity occurs in all times and places, regardless of the culture. Although one would expect to find pneumonia or measles anywhere in the world, the effect of different social settings might be to alter the expression of madness so much that no illness recognisable to modern psychiatrists as schizophrenia would be found in exotic times and places. In this chapter I take some glimpses back into history to examine the forms of madness that existed in earlier times.

Ancient Greece

Much of our concept of the nature of man and his place in society has been taken from Ancient Greece, especially from the time of the flowering of the culture of 5th century (BC) Athens, by means of a continuing cultural tradition through the duration of the Roman Empire and its influence on the Church to mediaeval, Renaissance and modern times. Therefore, the plentiful evidence relating to strange behaviour, mental disorder and madness in Ancient Greece is of particular interest.[44, 171, 200]

In the tragedies, written by dramatists in the 5th century BC, but portraying the characters of the ancient myths, madness is shown as occurring when the hero is overwhelmed by intolerable emotion. Orestes, who murdered his mother in revenge after she had killed her husband, Agamemnon, is overcome by remorse, and neglects to eat or wash. He is seen in a wildly unkempt state and when addressed replies that the problem is 'conscience'. Thus far, we see great intensity of emotion without any suggestion that it amounts to mental abnormality. However, among the various accounts is that of Euripides, which portrays him as seeing hallucinations and illusions in the form of dragons when the cattle are lowing and the dogs barking. Orestes was certainly supposed to be abnormal in his appreciation of reality, and his behaviour is far outside customary limits when, for example, he attacks the cattle with his sword.[231]

Ajax, in Sophocles' play of that name, breaks down under the intensity of his wounded pride. His proud self-sufficiency had already led him to live in a tent apart from his colleagues before he contested with Odysseus for the great prize of the arms of the slain Achilles. Odysseus was adjudged to have won, and Ajax flew into a towering rage, storming away to the hills intending to kill the other generals. Anger was honourable and expected, but when his pride makes him so arrogant and lawless, the goddess Athene humiliates him by driving him mad. He runs amok among the cattle and dogs, killing them, talking to shadows about Agamemnon, Menelaus and Odysseus, and laughing about how he had avenged himself. Later he comes to his senses in his tent, realises what he has done, and is silent (later still, he kills himself). 'The illusions of injured pride became the illusions of real madness' (Bowra[18]).

Madness is common in the tragedies, but there is no complete theory of its causes: Oedipus is in as desperate a situation as Orestes, and he acts desperately – he blinds himself – but not insanely. He still grasps reality without distortion or misinterpretation, and his behaviour does not transgress what is understandable. What is clear is that the heroes who are shown as breaking down do so in deeply personal emotional crises, the attribution of causes to the furies or deities scarcely detracting from the strong sense of individual tragedy: these divine influences are in intense relationship with the victims and can readily be seen as illuminating aspects of their dilemma.

A deeper analysis of a different view of madness was provided by Plato,[163] who maintained that, as well as the unproductive and uncreative form of the disorder, there was a divine form in which possession by a god could lead to inspiration and mystical insights. The Platonic division of man, traditional to this day, allocated rational attributes to the psyche, and emotion and impulse to the body.[164] Madness is impulsive, discordant, emotional and extreme; sanity is harmony, health, justice and reason. Madness occurs when the Greek ideal of moderation and self-knowledge is lost, as in the overwhelming emotion of the heroes of the dramas who lose their reason.

Hippocrates, the physician, writing not much earlier than Plato,[79] described a medical viewpoint that became the direct ancestor of psychiatry and the 'medical model' of madness. He pointed out the inevitable starting point and *raison d'être* of psychiatry: the role of the brain in the organisation of human behaviour. Emotions come from the brain, and disturbances of the brain can cause extraordinary and awesome behaviour, and make people mad. In particular, in a famous counterblast to superstition, Hippocrates emphasised that epilepsy was no sacred disease of possession by spirits, but was to be understood by knowledge of physiology, as were other illnesses. (However, the tradition of epilepsy as possession and not as physical illness survives strongly, through belief in the Bible, in some evangelical sects of Christianity to this day.) States of emotional disturbance were indeed disorders of balance and moderation, as in the view of the writers and philosophers, but the balance had physical roots in the brain and the hypothetical humours of the body (the bile, blood, phlegm and black bile, not now invoked in the physiology of emotion, although this usage still exists in the language – see the etymology of the adjectives of temperament: bilious, sanguine, phlegmatic and melancholic). Hippocrates probably reached his conclusions by observing cases of mental illness clearly secondary to physical disorder, such as delirium caused by high fever.

Hippocrates' treatment was also medical: drugs such as hellebore that had a reputation for affecting the state of mind; advice concerning diet and a sensible regimen of life to help restore balance; and education of the patient in the facts of his illness. There was no real attempt at psychological forms of treatment.

In the abundant records of the ancient world, are there accounts of individuals who were characterised as mad or whom in retrospect we would regard as suffering from a recognisable schizophrenic illness?

In the search for non-fictional accounts of mentally deranged individuals, the earliest examples are found in the histories written by Herodotus.[73]

Cambyses, the king of Persia from 530 BC, was prone to violent rages in which his behaviour was so extraordinary that it was generally agreed to be the result of mental disorder. He lost his temper at a religious festival, and, suspecting that he was being humiliated, 'ordered the priests of the god to be whipped, and stabbed a bull sacred to Apis so that the animal died'. This blasphemy and ridicule of religious rites could only be attributed to madness by the people of the time, and theories of the cause included a divine or psychological explanation – that it was a punishment for his impieties – and a medical one, that he was physically abnormal, possibly with life-long epilepsy. Certainly to modern eyes he appears to have had unusually violent tempers rather than mental illness.

In Sparta, there was another abnormal king, Cleomenes,[73] who was long regarded as bordering on insanity. When he started hitting with his sceptre anyone he met, he was put in the stocks despite his distinguished position. One day he managed to persuade his guard to give him a knife, and he then slashed himself repeatedly until, some time after wounding his stomach, he died. At the time, the explanations for his madness included the opinion that it was a divine punishment for his many blasphemous actions, such as interfering disgracefully with the pronouncements of the Delphic oracle and cutting down a sacred grove; Herodotus' point that Cleomenes had always been eccentric to the verge of insanity; and the Spartan view that he should have taken more water in his wine. These explanations suggest supernatural influences, life-long constitution, and physical causes of interest to the medical tradition, respectively. He does not seem to have been comparable to a modern patient suffering from schizophrenia.

I am indebted to George Rosen's scholarly *Madness and society*[171] for drawing my attention to the following examples.

One gentle madman wandered the streets of Alexandria day and night, naked in all weathers, derided by children and passers-by. A mob one day pretended to dress him up as a king and sat him in a mock court. Wandering in the streets and being an object of ridicule was commonly the fate of the mentally abnormal in Ancient Greece (and until recently, in all places throughout the ages), although many, especially the better-off, were sheltered and supervised within their families, whose responsibility to do this is mentioned by several authors. This man was recognisably abnormal, but his illness might not necessarily have been a forerunner of present-day schizophrenia, for we are not told if he had been able to speak at any time, whether he had always been simple (he might have been congenitally mentally handicapped), or if he declined into dementia and died (he might have had a slow cerebral illness).

Dionysius[175] of Syracuse was a brutal, merciless tyrant, suspicious about plots against his life. He used to write plays and submitted his compositions for the drama contests. After one humiliating judgment on one of his plays, he began to accuse even his friends of plotting against him out of envy, and many were executed on false charges. These are paranoid psychopathological symptoms, found in transient states and in schizophrenia, so his behaviour has a familiar ring to the modern psychiatrist.

Not very long afterwards, from the 4th century BC, Rosen cites the interesting case of an Athenian named Thrasyllus, who constantly frequented the Piraeus because he believed that all the ships coming into and leaving the port belonged to him. He kept track of them, noting their cargoes and destinations, and when a ship returned safely he rejoiced at the wealth it brought him. After his recovery, Thrasyllus clearly recalled his previous condition, asserting that he had never been happier than when he was deluded.[175] His recovery excludes the possibility of senile or other brain disease. He must have suffered from a recognisable mental illness: mania or schizophrenia, as described in modern textbooks.

A more detailed account exists concerning Menecrates,[176] a doctor from Syracuse in the 4th century BC. Menecrates claimed to be divine, added the name Zeus to his own, and collected an entourage of patients whom he had cured of mental illness. When he undertook the treatment of a patient, he did so on the condition that, if cured, the patient would become his follower and obey him in all matters. He had these acolytes dressed as the lesser gods of the pantheon, while he himself was Zeus, in a purple robe with a gold crown and sceptre. Menecrates may not have been insane. Although he could represent, in modern terms, a case of well adjusted schizophrenia with a rewarding role for his grandiosity, he may rather have been an eccentric but surely shrewd showman. There are some suggestions that his contemporaries regarded him as abnormal, but it is not clear if there was a consensus in favour of madness or cheek.

In the literature of Ancient Greece, some people are driven mad by the gods and the furies: they misidentify and kill their own children (Heracles); they wander distracted, prone to crazy talk, crazy dress (or nakedness), crazy avoidance of human contact, and crazy violence. Clearly this is a traditional, supernatural explanation of extraordinarily deviant behaviour. The gods and furies may be seen as personifications of outlawed aspects of the patient's personality for which he is not fully responsible. This explanation throws light on the philosophical ideal of moderation in all things, and knowing oneself. Rationality is sane; violence is mad.

A medical philosophy was present as a rival to the supernatural interpretation – and Plato[163] specifically mentioned both kinds of madness as being alternatives. Hippocrates decried superstition and attributions of sacredness to disease, yet the medical and magical–mystical theories were often intertwined – for example, many of the drugs employed were originally chosen for traditional superstitious reasons.

In the ancient world as in other times, the prevalent social themes are highlighted in the mental disorder of the people, especially in the famous cases and the literary stories that survive. The cult of the god of healing and ceremonies at the temple were orthodox institutions: Menecrates' extraordinary behaviour was in one sense a comment on them. When man is defined as a political animal (he lives in a *polis*, i.e. a Greek city state), a madman is one who wanders away from civilisation into the wilds. When the philosophical ideal is moderation and rationality in a world with capricious gods, fates and furies, the man who fails to conform explodes into mindless violence, as does Ajax.

The Old Testament

Among the ancient writings of the Hebrew people are many accounts of striking behaviour. In particular, I shall be concerned with the institution of prophecy in Palestine and with the lives of some of the prophets.[172]

My first example is Saul, whose extraordinary unstable actions caused his contemporaries to wonder whether he was afflicted by madness. At a time of mental exaltation after he had been anointed king, 'he prophesied among the prophets, then the people said one to another: what is this that is come unto the son of Kish? Is Saul also among the prophets?'[179]

On another occasion he took off his clothes and prophesied naked for a day and a night. More disturbing were his violent moods and uncontrolled rages when it was believed that he was tormented by an evil spirit: he attacked David because he brooded that he might supplant him, and another time set upon his own son Jonathan with a spear.

Kingship was a holy gift, the king being the Lord's anointed one. Ecstasy and prophecy also betokened a spirit from the realm of the divine, and the unpredictable uncontrolled outbursts of the prophet in his pronouncements were themselves evidence of a new dimension, inexplicable in purely human terms. The references to Saul's outbursts as being periods when the *evil* spirit from the Lord was upon him show that this was a way in which mental disorder was understood. Rosen, after a full discussion of Saul's case, wrote:

> Thus, it appears quite clear that among the ancient Israelites a significant objective criterion of mental disorder was the occurrence of impulsive, uncontrolled and unreasonable behaviour. Apparently, this was the basis for characterising prophets as madmen, since prophets did do strange things and acted peculiarly, inspiring awe and fear in some people and scorn in others. Prophetism and various phenomena associated with it are therefore of importance for an understanding of the limits within which the ancient Israelites viewed peculiar, eccentric behaviour as socially acceptable, and which thus also defined the boundaries of the psychopathological.[173]

Saul was a man of intense moods, including depression and brooding as well as outbursts of anger. He was under great pressure in leading the Israelites through a time of revolt and wars of survival, and his proud soul also had to acknowledge a bitter humility before Samuel, who had anointed him but later repudiated him.[179] Before the crucial battle his doubts increased to the point at which (in disguise, because he had himself expelled the witches and wizards from the land), he consulted the witch of En-dor, who prophesied his doom. In the final battle, he fought to the point of exhaustion and then killed himself.[179] In the Bible, the cause of Saul's disorder is seen as an evil spirit sent as punishment for sin; it was 'treated' with music therapy from David and his harp. We can see that he was a tormented, unstable leader of his times; the frequent modern diagnosis of epilepsy seems inaccurate, unnecessary and insensitive.

Prophecy was a traditional institution in Palestine and in neighbouring areas, just as analogous states of ecstasy and shamanism have been described in many peoples. The prophets, sometimes acting in groups, played a public and respected part in the religious and political life of Israel, recalling the errant people to respect for the ways of the Lord, exhorting the kings to patriotic fervour and galvanising them on the field of battle, predicting and proclaiming future disaster, and announcing the Lord's message. However, their behaviour was extraordinary not only to us but also to the people of the time, as they fasted, wandered, entered trances to speak the Lord's messages, donned sackcloth and ashes, and emphasised their message in symbolic mime. Zedekiah put horns on his head; Isaiah wandered naked and had visions from the Lord.[179]

Frequently, the pressure of the public role of prophecy and the intensity of their spiritual crisis as mere human and fallible vessels with a divine message drove the lone prophets to the verge of insanity, and there are frequent references to how bizarre their behaviour could be. Yet they were not disabled, not incomprehensible, not ignored. They did not even induce their prophetic states by music, dancing and drinking: the ingredients in the final result were the gifted moral, political and poetic stature of the individual in the crisis of his time, and the tradition of prophecy. Great visionaries led their people to purer distillations of their religious and moral beliefs, and Amos, Jeremiah, Isaiah and the unnamed writer of the later portions of the book of Isaiah have left us some of our greatest religious poetry.

There is no objective criterion for the 'normality' of states of ecstasy, prophecy and possession. It depends on the way the contemporaries of the prophet judge his behaviour, and not at all on the framework used by 20th-century psychiatrists to diagnose schizophrenia. Thus Benedict stated:

> It does not matter what kind of 'abnormality' we choose for illustration, those which indicate extreme instability, or those which are more in the nature of character traits like sadism or delusions of grandeur or of persecution, there are well described cultures in

which these individuals function at ease and with honour, and apparently without danger or difficulty to the society.

The most notorious of these extreme states is trance and catalepsy [inordinate maintenance of posture or physical attitudes[78]]. Even a very mild mystic is aberrant in our culture. But most peoples have regarded extreme psychic manifestations not only as normal and desirable, but even as characteristic of highly valued and gifted individuals.[12]

A prophet exploits the human potentiality for possession and trance to create sublimely and utterly personally:

What such a person sees and hears . . . is a product of subconscious material and processes, the result of ideas of reflection, of previous religious experiences, and of deeply rooted tendencies of his being worked through to a greater or lesser degree in the unconscious mind, and rising to the level of consciousness so that it seems to him to come from outside himself. A prophetic oracle or a religious revelation comes through the mediation of personal consciousness, but its occurrence and content are related to a specific socio-cultural milieu. In our time we distinguish sharply between objective and subjective phenomena. Hearing a voice where there is no visible speaker, or having a vision which is unrelated to the normal environment, is generally attributed to some unusual psychological condition of the individual who has these experiences. For the ancient Israelites such an explanation was not available. Experiences such as visions and auditions were explicable within the traditions of a theocratic community where religious capacities were venerated. God was the source of these experiences, a view consistent with previous beliefs of long standing.[174]

The finest example in the search for a case of schizophrenia in Biblical times is that of Ezekiel, the prophet, who lived in the 6th century BC.[51]

Ezekiel, a priest, recorded the exact time and day when 'the heavens were opened', and he saw 'visions of God', whose message was expressly for him. Thereafter he experienced visions, messages and close personal communion with God on innumerable occasions which he reported. He described scenes replete with symbolic meaning: he saw four creatures in human shape, with four faces and four wings, calves' feet, 'and they sparkled like the colour of burnished brass'. He saw wheels, and wheels within wheels, 'and the noise of their wings like the noise of great waters, as the voice of the Almighty'. A sapphire throne surrounded by brilliant rainbows appeared in the heavens, and

Ezekiel knelt down and received his commission to go to the people of Israel.

A book in a scroll was handed down to him with orders to eat it. He did so, and it tasted as sweet as honey.

Ezekiel was 'astonished' for 7 days and then received further instructions on his mission. He drew Jerusalem on a tile as a sign to the people, and then lay on his left side for 390 days to represent the years of the iniquity of the house of Israel, and on his right side for 40 days to represent the years of the iniquity of the house of Judah. When eating and drinking, he adopted rituals of a kind that were strictly taboo, baking his bread using human dung. He cut off his hair and divided it into three portions, burning one, chopping one up with a knife and scattering one in the wind (to symbolise death from pestilence and famine, death by the sword, and the scattering of the tribes of Israel, respectively). He was told to smite his head, stamp his foot and prophesy. The elders consulted him and then he heard the word of the Lord, delivering it in a ringing eloquence still heard down the subsequent centuries, with exhortations, symbols and allegories.

Sudden communion with God and the reception of a revelatory message is, of course, well known in religious conversion. Psychiatrists also describe the 'primary delusional mood' in schizophrenia, when the patient experiences a feeling of uncanny foreboding and an atmosphere heavy with significance, before suddenly realising with instantaneous, compelling certainty that there is some meaning of great significance to him. The revelation may seem banal to outsiders, though quite the opposite to the person experiencing it.

Ezekiel's call to be a prophet was similar in form, with symbolic visions, and his life was changed unshakeably from that moment. His symbolic actions with his hair and his posture are similar to the peculiar actions and postures of present-day schizophrenic patients, for which they often have a symbolic, albeit fragmentary, explanation, when they choose to reveal it afterwards.

The similarities between the two classes of phenomena, the religious and the schizophrenic, are that in each there is formed a belief with overwhelming explanatory power and concomitant pregnant meaning for the subject. Mystery is clarified, problems solved, and life explained. The primary delusion of the schizophrenic is a distorted pathological version of the process of the formation of a cherished belief, cherished because of its comforting explanatory power in both the normal and schizophrenic person. It is pathological in form because it is peculiar, unique to the patient and regarded as bizarre by all other people; and pathological in setting because it occurs in a disabled person who is losing or has lost his ability to think and live his own life.

However close the similarities, the differences are also very great: although Ezekiel's visions, pronouncements, and their symbolism are doubtless unique in that they are expressions of an individual human being, they are not bizarre or incomprehensible to his hearers. Far from being disabled, ill, shut in his own world and shunned as an insignificant eccentric, he was an inspiring public figure whose experiences led him, after personal struggles for commitment and courage, to influence the religion, morals and destiny of a 'stiffnecked' people. He mediated between the moral world and the life of the people of Israel. He was a prophet, doubtless a fanatical one who lived on what Graham Greene called 'the dangerous edge of things', in this case between sanity and psychosis. A prophet may be a madman, depending on the definition of madness, but he is not a schizophrenic if schizophrenia is a disablement of the normal functioning of mental capacity.

The Middle Ages

I shall not consider madness and schizophrenia in the annals of Roman civilisation and in the Dark Ages in Europe. The tradition of Greek medicine was attenuated but never lost, even though in the Dark Ages much of its survival was attributable to the Arabian medical schools. Its influence is best considered from the Middle Ages onwards. The religious, mystical and superstitious side of the Greek view of mental disorder had no direct descendant. In the remainder of this chapter I shall confine myself, for convenience and interest, largely to England.

The Middle Ages saw the establishment of a central administration, a complex and continuous legal system, and nearly all-pervasive Catholicism, the influence of the Church being assisted by its close identification of interest with that of the State. The scarcity of books, the transmission of learning in Latin, the difficulties of travel, the near-compulsory church attendance, and the scarcity of adherents to other religions, except for a handful of Jews, all intensified the domination of the Catholic church over the official, and a large part of the popular, philosophy. With the development of scientific enquiry at only an embryonic stage, it is not surprising that even dissenters from the main tradition, and folk beliefs that were not absorbed by it, were usually concerned with religion and heresy, and the development of beliefs in demons, magic and witchcraft.

It was the Church, therefore, that provided the religious mode in the understanding and treatment of mental disorder, which was thought to be caused by external influences, stigmatised as the devil, favourable but unexpected changes in the condition being attributed to divine grace, intercession, conversion, visitation in visions, and infliction of the holy stigmata. Healing cults were officially instituted at shrines such as those of St Bartholomew's in London, St Thomas à Becket in Canterbury, and the resting place of the body of King Henry VI at Windsor, as described later.

Nevertheless, the rational, professional, medical approach to mental disorder that was attempted in the Middle Ages was never negligible, and developed considerably during the period. Most historians of psychiatry have been so profoundly out of sympathy with that age that they have overestimated the irrationality and underestimated the strength of the struggling medical endeavours.

However, Clarke wrote:

The professional medical formulations, whatever their shortcomings for later readers and the size of their debt to the past, did represent a considerable collective intellectual construction; and the sections of texts which dealt with what we should mostly call psychiatric disorders give evidence of much struggling thought at times towards sensible solutions.[27]

Some of the textbooks of the time circulated widely: the compilation by Bartholomaeus Anglicus, a monk who wrote in about 1260, was widely known. Others often discussed were those of Gilbertus Anglicus and Bernard de Gordon.[30, 107, 156]

These books were full of material based on the Greek medical tradition, and did not express any preoccupation with demons and evil spirits, mention of which was rare before the 14th century, only becoming common from the late 15th. There are attempts at a rational pathology, with classification of maladies in accordance with a supposed origin in the unbalanced disposition of the four humours or in disorders of the ventricles of the brain (a largely spurious anatomy based on animals and ancient work).

Different syndromes, such as 'mania' and 'melancholia', were described, but with little impression of systematic observation of patients. Functional mental illness, occurring in the absence of gross physical illness, was recognised by these writers, who distinguished mania and melancholia as psychological disturbances 'without fever'. Epilepsy, despite Hippocrates' famous refusal to countenance it as a sacred disease, remained the condition with which the rational tradition had most difficulty, supernatural explanations of spirit possession still being mentioned. Over the whole field of mental disorder, it is clear that, as in other times and places, the supernatural and rational traditions both flourished, rational explanations greatly predominating among the doctors, and supernatural attributions to witches, astrological influences and demons being not so uncommon among the simple people. The clergy probably adopted an intermediate position that was less demonological than is attributed to them in many histories of medicine.

The difficulties in reaching a coherent body of knowledge must have been enormous, and we can sympathise with our forebears, because we in our turn do not find it easy to define boundaries between normal, mad, bad and sad behaviour, despite our knowledge of anatomy, physiology, pathology and psychology. In earlier centuries, the distinctions had to be made among illness, about which little was known, social disturbance, and crime or heresy, with drastic and different action required depending on which diagnosis was made.

The development of special provision for mental disorder in the law of mediaeval England illustrates further the social philosophy of the time. From the 13th century, when the law on the right and duty of the crown to protect the property of 'natural fools' was passed, there was a steady development in the recognition of the need for, and actual provision of, special arrangements for the mentally abnormal. Neugebauer[156] examined the unpublished records of inquisitions held to determine whether an individual was a lunatic or an idiot, and found that the hearings had a matter-of-fact tone with common-sense criteria for the impairment of a person's legal and social competence. Moreover, the theories of the causes of the conditions invoked physical and psychological bases of mental illness, with no supernatural explanations. Ignorance, and the absence of apparent cause, were expressed by a standard formula, 'by the visitation of God', which persists in legal formulae to this day and was certainly no token of preoccupation with the supernatural. In studying many cases, Neugebauer found only one supernatural explanation: a case of mental handicap that mentioned 'the snares of evil spirits'. So, official and establishment explanations of mental illness were rarely supernatural in the Middle Ages, although popular ones doubtless were often so.

The mentally ill remained very largely at home, or at least within the community at large, sometimes wandering. Hospitals for the sick became more widespread, but their charters show that they often specifically excluded the mentally deranged, this in itself suggesting the existence of a separate category for that disorder. Although institutional provision for mental patients began to a very small extent from the 13th century, at about the same time as in other European countries, it remained very scanty indeed until the 17th century, while there was no known continuous provision in a town outside London until the early 18th century.[1,29]

Some insane cases were seen and accommodated briefly at the

shrine of St Bartholomew from 1123, but this may not have amounted to specialised care. The first proper mental hospital may have been the Stone House near Charing Cross, from 1377, because there is a reference to six patients having been transferred from there to Bethlem in 1403.[28] The mention of these madmen is the first reference to mental patients in institutions, after which there is a further mention of incurable patients in 1451, and Bethlem Hospital has a continuous history, as an institution on different sites, from that time until this day.

A series of case histories has survived of people who went to the shrine at the tomb of Henry VI at Windsor in 1484 and in succeeding years, in the hope of miraculous cures.[31] Depositions of cures were written down, in order to collect evidence for canonisation, and were translated into Latin. We can look in Clarke's summaries to see whether there are any descriptions that sound like the schizophrenia of the 15th century, seen through the mediaeval context and interpretation of the disturbances. Mention of the 'ancient enemy' was still being made, with descriptions of the devil going about seeking whom he might devour, but Clarke suggests that the devil was a much less literal bogey than he had been earlier in the Middle Ages, and was more often 'a metaphor for the state of mind of peccant or deranged humanity'.[31]

The brief stories mainly describe visions, and dramatic changes in disabling illnesses, and none of the pilgrims sounds schizophrenic. Clarke says: 'There are no obvious chronic psychotics in the series, and they would not be expected since recovery is a requisite for inclusion.'

Clarke also gives a detailed account of the illness of King Henry VI,[32] and I have adapted his fascinating description in order to make it resemble more closely a psychiatric case history.

The future King Henry VI was 8 months old when his father died. He was brought up by the ladies of the court, in effect without parents, and had no brothers or sisters. With regard to the family history, Clarke points out that his father, Henry V, was stable and successful; his mother, Catherine, shallow but normal; and that his paternal grandfather, Henry IV, was probably well integrated until he suffered a personality change with reserve and suspicion in old age, and some unexplained long comas. However, the grandfather on his mother's side was the notorious Charles VI of France, who was energetic as a young man but became prone to episodes of very peculiar and undignified behaviour for over 30 years of his later life, sometimes rushing wildly about and talking obscurely, and at other times neglected and verminous, having to be forcibly washed. He became utterly impoverished in personality.

King Henry was on a judicial tour in July 1453, at the age of 31, when he was taken ill, as far as we know, with hardly any warning signs. The course of his life is known to have changed completely for the next year and a half, because there are reports of his being severely withdrawn, inaccessible to conversation, and consequently incapable of any active government of the country. He was described as being silent, apparently out of touch with time and deficient in memory, and usually sitting in a slumped position. In September of that year, he gave the cross of office to the new Archbishop of Canterbury, but at the end of the year did not appear to know of the death of the previous primate.

The council appointed a medical commission of three physicians and two surgeons (one of the physicians, Arundell, is thought to have been master of Bethlem in 1457–8, so perhaps he was the equivalent of a psychiatrist). They were told to treat him in accordance with the best textbooks and from a list of standard physical treatments of the time, 'according to the advice of experienced doctors who have written on this type of case or who shall write'.

In January 1454, his infant son, who had been born in November 1453 during the illness, was brought to him for a blessing. After several attempts by the Duke of Buckingham and the Queen to attract his attention, it was recorded that one fleeting glance was obtained, but then his gaze become downcast again. In March, he had to be supported on being led to meet a deputation of peers. They came on pressing business of state and repeatedly begged him to answer them, but were without success – he gave 'no answer, word or sign'. The consternation about his condition was such that the Duke of York was made Protector on 27 March 1454. From November 1454, there are accounts of improvement, and by Christmas he had fully recovered and was catching up with the events that had passed him by.

He seems always to have been a passive, eccentric and remote man. He had always managed some detachment from affairs of state, and had elaborate religious rituals even for his times. He knelt immobile for long periods at prayer, and wore a hair shirt at feasts of the church. He forgave a man the treasonable act of stabbing him, and would not have him punished. He never swore. He was thought to be prudish about nakedness, and wore unorthodox clothes: farmer's boots, black shoes and gloomy green coats. Later in life he had visions of Christ during the Eucharist and heard the voices of the saints. Various contemporary accounts suggest that, even when well, he was regarded as unfit to rule because of his simple and childlike traits. There were long awkward silences during a ceremony in Westminster Abbey in 1459. At the second battle of St Alban's in 1461, 'the king was placed under a tree a mile away, where he laughed and sang'. He died in 1471 at the age of 49.

It is difficult to suggest that his condition could have had a physical basis, because, after his long static stupor and presumably serious illness, he recovered without relevant treatment to his old self, at least for a time. The only diagnosis at all reasonable in modern times is that of a catatonic schizophrenic illness with withdrawal into stupor and then recovery after some partial relapses. This is more likely than a severe depressive withdrawal, because had it been this, some mention of the king's melancholy mood would have been expected. His basic personality, with its dreamy withdrawal, religious preoccupation and aloofness, conforms to one variety of the modern category of schizoid personality, and this in itself is closely related to schizophrenia in frequency of breakdown into mental illness. That at least one of his grandparents was mentally ill adds further support to this conclusion. We can here detect, therefore, a reasonably typical case of schizophrenia over 500 years ago. The attribution of mental illness is not incongruous as it would have been in the case of Ezekiel: King Henry was disabled by an episode reasonably called illness from which he recovered. His contemporaries regarded him as seriously impaired, and summoned physicians to treat him.

The witchcraft persecution

It has become traditional for histories of psychiatry to discuss the great European witch-craze of the 16th and 17th centuries. Interesting as it is in the history of ideas, the obsession with witches is not in itself a psychiatric matter, although there is an area of overlap, since aspects of the craze can be used to illustrate group hysteria, and because some of the victims were mentally abnormal. However, most of them were *not* abnormal, and the accusers were normal people caught up in the ideas of the time. Although many of the victims in England were unpopular, cantankerous old women[146] they were not insane, nor accused of insanity. Accounts of the intellectual and social background can be found in the books by Cohn[33] and Trevor-Roper,[222] the former describing the situation as 'an unconscious revolt against a religion which, consciously, was still accepted without question'.

Renaissance and 17th century Britain

The ideas of the Renaissance questioned and divided the Catholic Church, undermined and rejected old rituals, and renewed interest in the astonishing ancient civilisation at the origins of our own. People had to absorb the surprise of learning of new worlds across the ocean.

Madmen still wandered at large through the cities and countryside, as there were hardly any public institutions to care for them. There was much discussion as to whether madness was on the increase in those turbulent times, but this concern is common to all ages, for people always think that their own is the most stressful age of change ever known. Certainly the writers of the age displayed the whole gamut of society, eccentrics, warts and all, in their work. It was the age not only of Shakespeare's plays, but of Jonson's *Volpone* and *Bartholomew fair* in England, and of Rabelais in France. In Spain, Cervantes wrote the adventures of Don Quixote, and one of Lope de Vega's plays, *'Los locos de Valencia'*, is actually set in a lunatic asylum.[42]

The medical books of the time were clear that the brain underlay mental disorder. Laurentius, in *The diseases of melancholy*,[46] stated that the 'principal seat of the soul is in the brain', and not in the heart as Aristotle had suggested (cf. Portia: 'Tell me where is fancy bred, or in the heart, or in the head?'[197]). Burton, in *The anatomy of melancholy* (the psychological and psychiatric reference book of the time, although the author was not a physician), also wrote of the brain as 'the dwelling house and seat of the soul'.[23]

Paracelsus, a Renaissance polymath who had many arcane and alchemical interests, and who speculated about symbolic parallels among man, his diseases and the cosmos, nevertheless wrote at times of psychiatry as a completely rational matter. In a statement in direct intellectual descent from Hippocrates' emphatic denial of the sanctity of epilepsy, Paracelsus was bold enough to aver:

> In nature there are not only diseases which afflict our body and our health, but many others which deprive us of sound reason, and these are the most serious. While speaking about the natural diseases and observing to what extent and how seriously they afflict various parts of our body, we must not forget to explain the origin of the diseases which deprive man of reason, as we know from experience that they develop out of man's disposition. The present-day clergy of Europe attribute such diseases to ghostly beings and three-fold spirits; we are not inclined to believe them. (Taken from the preface to *Diseases that deprive man of his reason*, written around 1525 but not published until 1567.[158])

Treatment was managed as well as possible on an *ad hoc* basis in the absence of institutions to help, with the sole exception of Bethlem Hospital (Bedlam) in London. Public concern for the sick would eventually lead in the 18th century to the foundation of hospitals, as well as other institutions for paupers, misfits and criminals.

In the literature of the time, characters suffering from insanity lose their reason and their ability to assess truth, and wander away from society (cf. Ophelia, King Lear and Edgar as Tom O'Bedlam – in real life, Toms O'Bedlam were ex-patients discharged to beg on the streets of London). They sing distractedly and they comment fragmentarily on their dilemma and on society from their elusive vantage point, from which they cannot be held responsible or challenged.

Sir Thomas More briefly described the real case of a man who had been discharged from Bedlam where he had 'by beating and correccion gathered his remembrance to him and beganne to come again to himselfe, being thereupon set at liberty'.[83] On his release, the man again became frenzied in public, and was noisy in church especially, to the great scandal of the congregation, at the time of the levitation of the host in Mass. More had the constables take him away, tie him to a tree and publicly beat him. This was thought to have stopped his troublesome behaviour (which might have been called schizophrenic or manic nowadays). The harsh treatment was not unusual for these times, and was not a reflection on More who was seen as the most kindly of men by those around him – 'a man of singular virtue' to his son-in-law and biographer, Roper.[169]

Another account of a mentally disturbed man is that of William Hackett, described by Keith Thomas in *Religion and the decline of magic*.[219] Hackett was an illiterate and bankrupt ex-serving man who had persuaded himself that he was the Messiah come to judge the world on God's behalf. In 1591, he threatened plagues unless immediate reformation took place. He must have been a fierce and magnetic person, and he succeeded in persuading two Puritan gentlemen to be his prophets and disciples, one for the task of judgment and one for mercy. Before a crowd in Cheapside, Hackett declared that the Privy Council should be reconstituted and that the Queen had forfeited her crown. He was arrested for treason, and was executed, although he believed that a miracle would save him at the last moment. Thomas says that there were many other 16th-century Messiahs and figures from the Book of Revelation.

In the 17th century, the religious ferment and ideological differences in Christianity threw up many strange sects espousing extraordinary and sometimes radical revolutionary beliefs. The political and social scene is vividly described by Hill in *The world turned upside down*.[75] Biblical texts were taken literally, especially if this served the end of social (or sexual) release and a new order. Among the religious zealots and fanatics it is hard to tell who was individually unbalanced and who was unremarkable in his milieu at the time. Rosen gives this example.[170] On 23 November 1649, Thomas Tany, a goldsmith who had taught himself Hebrew, announced that he was a Jew of the tribe of Reuben and must change his name from Thomas to Thereau John. He proclaimed that he had been sent to initiate the return of the Jews to the Holy Land where they would rebuild Jerusalem and the temple, with himself as high priest. He made tents with emblems of the tribes on them, and then made a great bonfire and burned the tents, together with his pistols and Bible. He protested violently when Oliver Cromwell was offered the title of king, yet on 30 December 1650, he claimed to be the Earl of Essex and heir to the throne. He was arrested and served a term in prison. His last recorded act was to build a small boat in which he set out for Holland 'to call the Jews there', and was probably drowned on the way. I have myself seen a schizophrenic patient who set out in a rowing boat from the south coast of England to row to India.

For a description of an ordinary case of insanity far from the public eye, I use Hunter and Macalpine's account of George Trosse, divine of Exeter, and what happened to him in 1656 when he was 25 years old.[84] He heard the voice of God telling him to humble himself, and he tried to do so, but the voice would not leave him alone and he was tormented by the temptation to kill himself. For days he lay in bed with eyes and lips closed on the instructions of the devil. He heard 'Night and Day many Voices and Discourses; which I attributed to Fairies, who I thought were in the Wall, and there convers'd and were merry together . . .'. People in doorways seemed to say to each other, 'Must he go yet further into Hell?' He struggled with friends who wanted to dress and move him, thinking they were devils. He was moved to a private madhouse and treated with 'physic, low diet and hard keeping', being at times fettered to the bed to prevent escape. In a few months he completely recovered.

Here the religious crisis proceeded to the disruption of mental illness when he lost the ability to judge reality, and to distinguish perception from imagination. Thus, he heard not a metaphorical voice of conscience, not a theologically orthodox voice of God or possibly devils and angels, but multiple voices, attributed to 'fairies', and laughing about him. Similar experiences are reported by schizophrenic patients today.

We still find Messiahs to this day from time to time; but it is a secular age and few of the fellow citizens of such a man are impressed by religious revelations. This in itself may make him unlikely to talk about his special status. However, if he does so, his family and neighbours will start to invoke our category, 'mental illness', and will send for the doctors. If he makes too much fuss, he will certainly be removed from circulation – to a psychiatric hospital ward. Yet dominant personalities with extraordinary beliefs can still attract followers: Jim Jones formed a community of American expatriates in the jungles of Guyana, and, when trouble from outside threatened, hundreds killed themselves on his orders. In California, Charles Manson persuaded his followers to commit murder and mutilation. In *When prophecy fails*[53] a small group is described who shared the belief of its woman leader that they had been chosen for rescue, at the imminent end of the world, by a flying saucer. In different circumstances, and if known to psychiatrists, such leaders might have been diagnosed as schizophrenics with grandiose delusional beliefs and possibly hallucinations of messages from God, or Venus in the case of the woman just described.

The 18th century

Perhaps the people became tired of religious enthusiasm. Outwardly there was prosperity for some in the 18th century, and colonial enterprise flourished abroad, but the occurrence of wars, the start of the Industrial Revolution in the second half of the century, the enclosure of common land, changes in the extended family and the centralisation of the population in the towns ensured continuing poverty and squalor for many, and vagrancy in town and countryside. Those who had the leisure to discuss ideas talked of the rational philosophy.

Locke had explained that man has no innate ideas, but is born with a clean slate of a mind on which to register and manipulate impressions from the sense organs.[142] This threw doubt on claims of blinding inner experience of the Godhead, and the theology of the time became rational in style. Voltaire was no Christian but a deist; Hume carried Locke's epistemological arguments further, and moreover was an atheist. Newton's grand explanatory theories had greatly reduced the need for the deity to intervene and cause the events of the universe: having created the universe and its laws, God need thereafter have a lesser role than had been assumed before.

The philosophers studied the mind, but not the mentally ill. Nevertheless, their theories affected people's views of insanity, at least those held by the educated members of society. When God is less in evidence in everyday life, being seen as an unmoved mover of the universe, and when the personal reality of the devil is no longer preached from the pulpit, madness is not attributed to demonic possession, holiness or any supernatural occurrence. It becomes an individual human phenomenon, a misfortune or weakness. Thus, although amongst simple people the attribution of awesome mysterious phenomena to witchcraft or devilish interference persisted, the more educated explained madness in terms of moral weakness and overindulgence (cf. *The rake's progress* by Hogarth, in 1733, which has a scene where the rake has reached Bedlam), and of a failure of the faculty of reason. There were also piecemeal disease theories provided by the doctors of the time, but there was as yet no medical category of mental disorder.

The level of theory in medical books remained rather primitive: Burton's *Anatomy of melancholy*[23] was still popular after over a century, and the four humours were still discussed. They were only abandoned very slowly, by way of their supposed influence on moods, passions, styles of thought and temperament, which then themselves became the object of study, a shade less abstract and closer to the patient who required help. There was much discussion of melancholia and its symptoms, and many doctors noted the coincidence of melancholic gloomy, apathetic states and frenzied overexcited periods in the same patients: presumably the manic-depressive psychosis of our 20th-century classification. Madness proper was distinguished from mental derangement caused by physical illness, usually 'fever'. Thus, Dr Thomas Willis stated: 'Melancholy is a madness without fever or frenzy, accompanied by fear and sadness.'[56] However, he was clear that it nevertheless somehow originated in the brain, and this has been the standard medical theory since that time.

Provision for the insane changed greatly during the 18th century, as a response to the needs of the victims themselves, but also because of the prevalent view of society that deviant individuals should be sent to institutions. This was the age that started to deal with awkward people by locking them away. There were too many Toms O'Bedlam begging and others aping them, too many vagrants, ne'er-do-wells and paupers of all descriptions swarming in the country, at least according to contemporary accounts. This was the age of Bridewell prisons and the foundation of public hospitals, although thousands of the insane were still to be treated with neglect and cruelty in private madhouses or, if more fortunate, were left with their own families. Foucault[56] dates 'the great confinement' in France from 1656, when the Hôpital Général was founded to take in the problem poor and the idle. However, confining ourselves to England, we find that after Bethlem, the next public provision for the mentally ill was not made until 1696 when The Corporation of the Poor Workhouse in Bristol (later St Peter's) created separate wards for lunatics, who were cared for and not merely confined and punished.[1] In 1713, the Bethel hospital was founded in Norwich, and in 1728 the new Guy's Hospital in London had a department for lunatics, and specifically undertook to care for incurable cases along with the more promising ones. In 1751, St Luke's was started by public subscription in London (and was intended to have facilities for teaching medical students), and asylums were opened in Manchester in

1766 and later on in other cities. The movement to open mental hospitals did not keep up with demand, and numerous private mad-houses sprang up during this period, often taking in pauper cases, the fees of which were paid by the public authorities who had no institution under their own control.[94, 159]

An insane patient of the time was Alexander Cruden, compiler of the concordance to the Bible, some details of whose story are given by Hunter and Macalpine.[85] He had long been an eccentric, but in 1739 his friends had him confined as insane to a private madhouse for three short periods. He had become unbalanced in his megalomaniac reforming zeal, calling himself 'Alexander the Corrector', after Alexander the Great, 'Corrector of the Morals of the Nation', and he petitioned Parliament for an official appointment to recognise his position. Similar cases can be seen today when schizophrenia develops in intelligent and morally zealous people: beliefs about a special mission may come to have delusional force, and are often accompanied by hallucinations of the voice of the Deity giving a special message. The ability to think and compose clear sentences and even books may be well preserved for many years, although it is often lost eventually.

The beginning of modern psychiatry

Late in the 18th century there occurred several events which are often taken as landmarks in the history of psychiatry, and as beginning a new era. Psychiatrists are accustomed to honour William Tuke, the Quaker who in 1792 founded the Retreat at York, and Philippe Pinel who in 1793 struck off the chains of the inmates of the Bicêtre asylum in Paris. The undoubted importance of their influence is not diminished by rival claims for priority in the treatment of lunatics in institutions with kindness and without mechanical restraint (Chiarugi in Italy may have been equally bold in 1788[61]). Changes were occurring in the ideas about insanity at this time, to which they contributed by their writings[161, 224] and actions.

It is agreed, by Rosen, physician and historian of medicine,[171] Foucault, historian of ideas,[56] and Scull, sociologist,[190] that the last quarter of the century saw the separation of mental disorder as an entity from the deviance of the mass of other non-conformers in society: the paupers, disabled and misfits in general. From being considered incomprehensible, irrational specimens, almost comparable to brute animals, and condemned on occasion to conditions unfit for any human being, the insane came to be regarded, in the official view at least, as disabled fellow-citizens, suffering from disease, and requiring decent medically supervised care, albeit firmly segregated from society in institutions. One influence in this change of view came from the King's famous illness.

King George III was popular with his subjects, and a highly religious, conscientious and abstemious man, who was devoted to his wife. In 1788, he suffered his first attack of insanity. Because of his political duties, for example that of chairing the Cabinet every week, his illness could not be hushed up: it was the major news for 4 months, and led to widespread discussion of the issues involved. Interest has continued to our time, with accounts from which I draw by Trench[221] and Macalpine and Hunter.[145] *

During his illness, the king was wildly excited, talking non-stop for days on end to the point of hoarseness and exhaustion. He was uninhibited, coarse and inappropriate in his speech and behaviour, to the great consternation of the court and the discomfiture of the distinguished society physicians called in to treat him. They failed, and a psychiatrist was sent for: he Reverend Doctor Francis Willis, an obscure madhouse keeper from Lincolnshire, who came with his son, three keepers and a straitjacket. Willis ruled the sick-room ruthlessly, and was drastic with straitjacket and physical treatment. The king had blisters applied, purges, emetics, and a meatless diet for weeks on end. Most of the doctors consulted had said that the condition was incurable, because it was insanity without delirium: that is, the king was not physically ill in the ordinary sense, but had gone insane. Willis said he would recover and, amid national thanksgiving, he did. The king's dignity and courage in returning to public life left a strong impression on the nation, as did the drastic physical treatment and restraints he had undergone, and there appeared a mass of pamphlets and books discussing the subject. However, later in life the king was to suffer relapses and years of mental illness.

In 1792, William Tuke, Quaker tea and coffee merchant of York, founded the Retreat in that city, after suspecting shameful conditions at the York Asylum, a subscription hospital that resisted visiting by outsiders. The Retreat catered for only 30 patients and care was conducted on religious and humane principles, the methods of management coming to be known as 'moral treatment'. Details can be found in *Description of the Retreat,* written by Samuel Tuke, grandson of the founder.[224] The Tukes believed that the violence of the

---

*The last two authors have argued against the plausible diagnosis of manic-depressive psychosis, claiming that the king suffered from porphyria, an extremely rare, hereditary metabolic disorder.[143,144] This diagnosis has become received wisdom among historians, but is not found convincing by many psychiatrists, including myself. However, this is not the point here.

insane had been greatly exaggerated, and was in any case made far worse by cruel treatment. The patients were so far as possible trusted to be of good behaviour, which was then rewarded, and when possible they mixed socially with the superintendent's family, went for walks and had suitable occupation and reading matter.

In 1793, Pinel, distinguished and scholarly physician, convinced the Governor of the Bicêtre, the public institution in Paris for the male insane and for other of society's problems, that the inmates could and should be cared for without chains. His account in *A treatise on insanity*[161, 205] shows how daring this was. The building was dauntingly unsuitable for his purpose, cramped, lacking baths, and with hardly any space for exercise. He was hampered by the inability to segregate the patients in groups according to the severity and stage of their illness.

Yet it was usually impracticable and undesirable to attempt the treatment of the insane in their families, because restraint under such conditions was constantly irritating and the patient could not be kept calm, with the result that few recovered. Moreover, patients admitted from home with a reputation for violence were often found to be calm and easily manageable in hospital, whereupon caution was needed to avoid premature discharge and consequent relapse at home.

So the imperfect public hospital had to be used, but Pinel urged, in modern vein, that when a new one was to be designed, the plans should be submitted to the medical staff for their approval.[205] In this alarming powder-keg of an institution, and not without considerable difficulties with alarmed lay authorities, the chains were struck off. The greatest vigilance was necessary to ensure that the staff did not continue any cruel practices or disobey the orders they had received that no man was allowed to strike a maniac even in his own defence. The problem of engaging suitable staff was solved by employing convalescent patients as servants. Violent behaviour decreased:

A degree of liberty sufficient to maintain order, dictated not by weak but enlightened humanity, and calculated to spread a few charms over the unhappy existence of maniacs, contributes in most instances, to diminish the violence of the symptoms, and in some to remove the complaint altogether.[161]

The energy and sincerity of 19th century reformers at their most vigorous was tremendous, and the results in many social fields were very remarkable. It is usual to praise them almost unstintingly, although they are presented cynically as highly paternalistic controllers of the poorer classes by Scull in *Museums of madness*,[190] which piles up evidence for that author's radical sociological viewpoint. He sees the movement for lunacy reform as inspired by social change and the need to suppress deviants. From this point of view, the rampant capitalism of the economic system forced the poorest classes to be preoccupied with working for wages, so that awkward, disabled, unproductive members of society could not be tolerated as harmless lunatics at large, as had been the custom in past centuries. The misfits could not be permitted to be too visible: workhouses were built, and then the asylums, ostensibly for cure but, in fact, it was no coincidence, in this view, that they became dumping grounds for all manner of social derelicts, who rarely returned to life outside.

In 1807, a Select Committee of the House of Commons was appointed to inquire into the state of criminal and pauper lunatics in England. It heard evidence, especially from prison reformers such as Sir George Onesiphorus Paul of Gloucestershire, about the conditions 'revolting to humanity' of pauper lunatics in workhouses. These people were often chained in filthy, damp cellars, and received no care or compassion, although they were presumably afflicted in their insanity even more greatly than the sane inmates by the grim prevailing conditions. It also became clear that no one knew, nor could anyone find out, how many lunatics there were in England, even in public care. Written returns from the counties were obviously guesses or designed to maintain that the problem did not exist locally, and no one knew how many might be confined privately with no supervision. The County Asylum Act to implement the recommendations of the Committee was passed in 1808, allowing the magistrates to raise money to construct and maintain asylums, but not compelling them to do so. Only a handful were built.

In 1815, another Select Committee was set up to examine evidence on the state of the provision for lunatics, and the result was a thorough consideration of Bethlem, York Asylum, St Luke's Hospital in London, the new Nottingham Asylum, private madhouses and workhouses. At Bethlem, the public already knew of scandalous conditions and efforts to cover up in the face of their concern. Quiet and coherent female patients had been kept chained and naked. The case was described of William Norris, who had been continuously chained to a wall for 9 years, unable to roll over when lying down or to move more than one step away, and who was in any case weak and dying of tuberculosis.[95, 191] At York Asylum, a resourceful reformer had with great persistence found a hidden group of cells smeared with faeces, and a stinking room 'twelve feet by seven feet ten inches in which there were thirteen women who . . . had all come out of those cells that morning'.[96] At Nottingham, the development of the new public asylum had met with many difficulties, including its novelty, the economy forced by the authorities and the fact that it was over-crowded from the very first year.

In the asylums, small numbers of staff, in crowded conditions, endeavoured to prevent the escape of patients, for which penalties were laid down. Therefore, it is hardly surprising that mechanical restraint remained common, and in 1839 when Conolly abolished it at Hanwell Asylum, he was able to make obsolete 300 handcuffs and leglocks as well as sundry other items of leather and iron-ware.[168]

Medical views on mental illness were also changing during this period, albeit slowly and with very little advance in the actual knowledge of causes and effective treatment. The first reforms at the end of the 18th century had sprung from a more experienced clinical approach that was beginning to be shown by some members of the medical profession, as may be seen in Dr William Battie's *A treatise on madness*, published in 1758. His definition of madness is a clear one, and linked to the concept of delusion. Thus, he wrote: '. . . deluded imagination . . . is not only an indisputable, but an essential character of madness . . . That man and that man alone is properly mad, who is fully and unalterably persuaded of the existence or the appearance of any thing, which either does not exist or does not actually appear to him, and who behaves according to such erroneous persuasion.'[86] Hunter and Macalpine comment: 'His Treatise on Madness was not only the first with this title, but also the first by a psychiatrist who could draw on his experiences with a large number of patients.'[86]

After moral treatment had been urged and demonstrated by Chiarugi, Tuke and Pinel, others had to continue the work, and they are also worthy of memory, for the struggle to minimise and abolish mechanical restraint of the patients was long-lasting. In England, Tuke at the Retreat could be disregarded by those unwilling to trust his methods, on the grounds that he took selected cases: in a public asylum with staff of doubtful quality, where pauper lunatics, the dregs of society, were taken from the workhouse, the methods of the Quakers could be considered utopian. So, it was of the greatest importance when Dr Robert Gardiner Hill at Lincoln Asylum stated that he had abolished restraint by the principles of moral treatment: by separating patients with different degrees of disturbance from each other; by unremitting close observation of behaviour to prevent impending incidents; by occupation; by 'enough strong attendants well paid and of good character'; and by kindness. He wrote that, 'In a properly constructed building, with a sufficient number of suitable attendants, restraint is never necessary, never justifiable, and always injurious, in all cases of lunacy whatever.'[76, 132]

Dr John Conolly visited Hill at Lincoln, and in 1839, when he became Physician Superintendent of Hanwell Asylum, the largest in the country, he abolished all mechanical restraint. He faced great difficulties in pushing through such a daring policy, as did Hill (who was forced to resign from Lincoln), and some of his other ideas, ahead of his time, foundered. He started classes for literacy and sought as many occupations as he could find for the patients; and he pressed for the establishment of training for the attendants in methods of caring for the mentally ill.[97]

Although the humanity of doctors of the calibre of Gardiner Hill and Conolly cannot be faulted, they had to work with very simple concepts of the cause of insanity. Conolly himself was blind to social and psychological causes, and attributed symptoms and the whole condition to purely hypothetical physical influences. Thus, he stated that, 'To be entirely divested of dress seems a favourite fancy of many lunatics when first attacked; it probably arises from a morbid sense of heat, or from some uneasiness in the skin.' No mention of nudity in inappropriate places as a desperate protest against society's rules. 'The idea of all objects being impure or dirty would seem to depend on some disorder in the peripheral terminations of the nerves of the surface, the idea of being galvanized or poisoned often arises from a coppery taste connected with disordered digestion . . .' and so on.[35]

The new profession of asylum doctors explained that the running of asylums was a medical matter, and that moral treatment – usually agreed to be a good thing, but not a particularly medical expertise – was to be combined with physical treatment of a medical kind with sedative drugs and purgatives, for the best results to cure insanity. It was thought that more patients could be cured if they could be admitted at an earlier stage of their illness, and it was emphasised that admission to the asylum was a humane measure not only for those in workhouses, but even for patients living at home with their families. This was a suggestion that needed cogent support, because the asylums were known to be grim institutions with bleak regimes, and there was no tradition of sending afflicted relatives away.[192] Gardiner Hill wrote of 'the improbability . . . of an insane person's regaining the use of his reason except by removing him early to some Institution for that purpose'.[77]

In 1845, two Acts were passed, finally making it mandatory for counties to erect asylums for the poor. These followed a specially ordered nationwide survey by the Metropolitan Commissioners in Lunacy, which had shown great differences in standards around the country, and yet again some shocking conditions with many pauper lunatics in crowded special sections of workhouses. As a result of the Acts, new asylums were built, and were rapidly overfilled. Extensions were built, and more asylums. Their great size depressed morale and the doctors protested, but still the patients came. The average size of public asylums rose from 116 patients in 1827 to 1221 in 1930.[99] (Many mental hospitals have had over 2000 patients, and the largest ever had 14 200.[148])

Neglected insane people were found in the workhouses and at large, and were sent to the asylums, but undoubtedly these institutions were used also, because they existed, as places for the disposal of many of society's other misfits. This tendency continues to this day, when many of the places in our mental hospitals are occupied by the senile, who need nursing somewhere (the problem of the need for provision for the senile was already being reported with dismay in the 1850s[193]).

The deprived life in a typical asylum is well described in Hunter and Macalpine's *Psychiatry for the poor, 1851 Colney Hatch Asylum; Friern Hospital 1973.*[87] In 1854, the official report stated 'Mechanical restraint is not resorted to in this asylum, seclusion in rooms padded with hair and canvas being adopted in instances of paroxysmal and dangerous violence, during the continuance of which medical and moral treatment is also pursued to bring the case to a favourable issue.'[88] However, in 1861, not enough patients were given an occupation; few were taken for walks; there were no books and newspapers to read; mixing of the sexes on recreational occasions only occurred once a year; there were uncomfortable chairs, cold dormitories and too few blankets; the air was bad and the lavatories were smelly and inconvenient; and patients bathed together in the same bathwater.[89] Moral treatment had lost its way in the great asylums. There was little human contact between staff and patients; in the workshops of the hospital work was done at least as much to save money as to benefit the patients themselves; and classification in different wards to improve the patients' environment had become merely an exquisite exercise in degrees of deprivation.

In the 19th century, the result of our enquiry whether, among the tragic figures sent to the asylums, patients can be found suffering from the schizophrenia of modern psychiatry is perfectly clear: the insane commonly had typical schizophrenia, indistinguishable from the present-day condition.

In Pinel's book of 1801, many patients are mentioned briefly: one believed he was Mahomet; many had grandiose delusions of being kings and even deities, and had vivid hallucinations; one wandered about the hospital muttering and smiling to himself, but answered questions correctly; one was normal to talk to and in most of his behaviour, but always signed himself 'Christ'. These are some of the chronic schizophrenic patients of yesteryear.[205] I shall mention three famous examples.

The paranoid schizophrenic syndrome, with delusions of systematic persecution by enemies using a mysterious machine, is exemplified by Haslam's patient, the subject of the book published in 1810 with the informative title: *Illustrations of madness: exhibiting a singular case of insanity, and a no less remarkable difference in medical opinion: developing the nature of assailment, and the manner of working events; with a description of the tortures experienced by bomb-bursting, lobster-cracking and lengthening the brain. Embellished by a curious plate* (which shows the 'Air Loom' by which the patient's enemies influenced him).[71]

Daniel McNaughton, tried in 1843 for the murder by shooting of Mr Drummond, the private secretary to Sir Robert Peel, and acquitted on the grounds of insanity, also suffered from paranoid schizophrenia.[230] He was a wood-turner, a single and rather solitary man, who was highly intelligent and had tried to improve his education at the Mechanics' Institution in Glasgow. For several years he had believed he was persecuted: he thought that he was being watched and followed, and blamed for crimes he had not committed, by a conspiracy of Jesuits, and later Tories. He went to the authorities several times to beg for the persecution to be investigated and stopped. He found that the spies seemed to follow him even into his bedroom at night, and when he travelled abroad to get away from them, he noticed one peering at him as soon as he landed at Boulogne. He saw people in the street making signs about him: one carried straw which signified that he would go downhill and end his days on straw in an asylum. Sometimes he slept in the fields to shake off the spies. He called it all a 'grinding of the mind'. At the same time, witnesses who had mixed with him a good deal, including his landlady of a year and a half, described McNaughton as a retiring but normal man, completely unremarkable. He bought two pistols several months before the crime, and had been hanging around Whitehall for days. He fired one pistol, and was disarmed before he could shoot with the second. After his arrest he said, 'He shall not break my peace of mind any longer,' and explained that when he saw Drummond give him a look as he went by, all his sufferings and wrongs welled up in his mind. The unfavourable public reaction to the acquittal led later to the McNaughton rules, long used as the test of criminal responsibility in English law.

McNaughton at that time was 29 years old. He was sent to Bethlem, and to Broadmoor Asylum when it opened in 1864. He was a quiet patient, usually avoiding all other people as much as possible, speaking little, and at one period was forcibly fed when he tried to starve himself. He died in 1865, aged 52 years.

The third famous patient is Daniel Schreber, who published his own memoirs,[186] and whose case was discussed by Freud[58] in developing the psychoanalytic theory of paranoid thinking. Schreber's father was a doctor and an eccentric social reformer. He was the author of a successful book on medical gymnastics, and held extreme views on the upbringing of children, one of which was that they should be restrained in fearsome apparatus to ensure proper posture. The father's writings are used to good effect by Schatzman in his book *Soul murder*[180] to argue that Schreber's case neatly illustrates that schizophrenics' delusional beliefs and hallucinatory experiences refer obliquely but accurately to actual experiences in childhood at the hands of their parents (see Ch. 8). Schreber was a lawyer, happily married but deeply grieved by childlessness. At the age of 42, he was admitted to a psychiatric clinic for 6 months with 'hypochondriasis', but recovered completely, so that he returned to the bench as a judge after an interval of a year. He remained well for 8 years until 1893, when, at the age of 51, 6 weeks after promotion to the Court of Appeal in Saxony, he was admitted to Sonnenstein Asylum where he spent the next 9 years. His mental illness was very severe for at least the first 2 years, but later it remitted partially, so that his outward behaviour was much less abnormal, and he petitioned for and obtained his release. His later fate is not known.

He made notes on his state of mind even when very disturbed, and retained a remarkable ability to comment on his whole range of experiences, so that his memoirs are a unique document, a description by a very highly intelligent, well read man, trained to marshal argument, of an extremely severe psychosis. The material is very complicated and virtually impossible to summarise: the memoirs and the commentary by Macalpine and Hunter should be read by anyone interested in mental illness. Some of the themes concern Schreber's belief that God, by miracles and rays, acted on his body in an 'unmanning' process to turn it into a woman's. This caused feelings of voluptuousness, of female orgasm, and a conviction of having miraculously conceived. Voices talked to Schreber for years, coming, he believed, from transmigratory souls. People around were only apparently real, and were, in fact, 'fleetingly-improvised' men. There was a state of 'moonshine-blessedness'. He wrote: 'Scorpions were repeatedly put into my head, tiny crab or spider-like structures which were to carry out some work of destruction in my head. These had the nature of souls and therefore were talking beings; they were distinguished according to their place of origin as 'Aryan' and 'Catholic' scorpions. . . . Friendly souls always tended more towards the region of my sexual organs . . . whereas inimical souls always aspired towards my head, on which they wanted to inflict some damage, and sat particularly on my left ear in a highly disturbing manner.'[187]

At the end of the century, the asylums, already set in their ways, were further confirmed as bureaucratic institutions by the Lunacy Act of 1890, which contained a mass of provisions for documentation of admissions, and for certification by magistrates, designed to close all loopholes through which a sane man could be wrongly detained. However, the procedures hindered efforts at change and new styles of treatment: Kathleen Jones calls the period leading up to it and the act itself 'the triumph of legalism', and says that 'From the medical and social viewpoint, it was to hamper the progress of the mental health movement for nearly seventy years.'[98]

Also in the 1890s, in Munich, Kraepelin in his influential textbook of psychiatry,[105] introduced the modern classification of severe mental illness, since used in all psychiatric textbooks. Studying severely disturbed patients in the asylum, and giving very full descriptions based on his own extensive observation of the patients and the cause of their illnesses over many years, he described dementia praecox as an illness with typical features. The disturbance often started in adolescence (but by no means always), and there were hallucinations, delusions, withdrawal from the outside world, disruption of the process of thinking and logic, emotional disorders, and stereotyped changes in posture and movement. The illness was often very severe and long-lasting, leaving many patients changed for the worse from their previous selves, although a few recovered. Kraepelin speculated very little on causes, but expected physical factors to be found eventually. Certainly his stance is always felt to be detached and descriptive, that of the (by definition, sane) doctor observing the (insane) patients accurately, as is shown by Laing's pitiless exposé in *The divided self.*[113]

The term 'schizophrenia' for this illness was coined by Eugen Bleuler in 1911,[14] when he emphasised that there was a 'group of schizophrenias' for which the common factor was a splitting of psychic functions. He was prepared to use the label for a wider group of patients than Kraepelin's very disturbed ones, and he suspected that the causes would include, as well as the expected hereditary and biological ones, psychodynamic factors concerned with the conflicts in the patient's mind: this was the influence of the ideas of Freud, who was born in 1856, in the same year as Kraepelin.

Thus, with Kraepelin, Freud and Bleuler, we reach modern views of madness and schizophrenia.

Conclusion

There are plenty of descriptions of mad people in the literature and records of any age that we consider. However, the form of that madness is my present interest, and in particular whether there are any types which persist from age to age, comparable to the schizophrenia of present-day psychiatry.

It is clear that grandiose religious and political reformers with powerful drive and capacity for leadership, who are able, although precariously, to found and lead movements for years on end without mental breakdown, have been found in all the ages we have examined: Menecrates with his community; Hackett, Tany and Cruden in early modern England; Jones of Jonesville, Guyana, and the malignant Charles Manson of California, in our time. They distanced themselves from the ordinary thought of their contemporaries, and personal idiosyncratic preoccupations seem to have led them to all-explaining beliefs. Simpler and weaker people have banal and obviously crazy delusions; they break down and cannot manage their lives. Powerful personality, and good fortune in finding a niche in their contemporary society in which to develop their ideas, preserved these leaders, at least temporarily, from mental disorganisation into severe withdrawal, hallucinations and delusions.

Ezekiel, and George Fox, the founder of the Quakers, whom I mention in Chapter 3, were near to breakdown: without their extreme moral strength, and without audiences attuned to prophetic religious enthusiasm, they might have succumbed to their vivid experience of the divine. The same phenomena in lesser souls and materialistic times are the bread and butter of religious hallucinations in numerous schizophrenic patients who become unable to think clearly or look after their simplest daily needs.

The weaker who become withdrawn and alienated do not influence those around them: they cease altogether to communicate comprehensibly with others. Henry VI suffered this to an extreme extent, and it must be doubted whether he would have survived so long in a stupor had he not been the revered figure of the monarch; lesser citizens must surely have perished unless they had unusual care. The madman described by Sir Thomas More had been treated in Bethlem, and George Trosse, the churchman with the vivid fairy voices, was preserved from self-harm by unwilling incarceration in a private madhouse.

From the later 18th century onwards, we find cases that can easily be compared with those of modern times: some chronic schizophrenics in Pinel's Bicêtre; George III's manic-depressive illness; Haslam's man persecuted by a magic machine; McNaughton with fairly simple and Schreber with highly elaborate delusional and hallucinatory schizophrenic disorders.

The cases resemble schizophrenia the more closely as we come nearer to modern times: the culture is exerting its effect on one possible abnormal pattern of mental activity. The pattern includes withdrawal and unusual, idiosyncratic and abstract styles of thinking, together with a concern with hidden meanings. In the early stages, the reaction of people around makes a considerable difference to the outcome, as does the constitution of the person. An outstanding schizoid man in ancient Palestine was shaped by social expectations into being a mystical prophet of his people. A lowly citizen of Britain in the 20th century who fasts, prays and pronounces messages revealed to him from God is confronted by alarm in everyone around him, and only psychiatrists have a suggestion as to what to do with such a wayward man. His symptoms start being disabling and resembling those of schizophrenia. There is little divine madness, and no one moves over to make room for a mystic. We live in secular times.

6

Knowledge of causes (i) Physical causes

In this chapter and the next, I give a brief summary of what is known of the causes of schizophrenia from the medical, clinical and scientific tradition. This account is based on the speculations and research over the past 100 years of psychiatrists and of scientists in the biological and social sciences: in genetics, biochemistry, neurophysiology, pharmacology, psychology and sociology. For the majority of this time, psychiatrists and nurses were the only professional people to actually meet, study and try to help the patients; apart from the relatives concerned, no other group shared this close relationship until psychologists, occupational therapists and social workers joined the clinical team a few years ago.

The amount of research has been enormous, and it is recounted in similar ways in many books, especially those written as textbooks for psychiatrists. Therefore, this account will be confined to a selection of the main findings, although frequent references to the sources and to further reading are given. The fact that different definitions of schizophrenia have been used by different research workers has presented a problem. However, to avoid repetitive discussion on this point, the considerable area of common agreement on what is schizophrenia has sometimes been taken for granted, although at other times I allude to the problems of different diagnostic habits.

Heredity

It is common knowledge that insanity runs in families, and it has long been known that this is indeed the case for schizophrenia. Whereas about 1 per cent of the adult population will suffer from schizophrenia during the course of their lifetime, the frequency among the relatives of patients is far higher. The parents, brothers, sisters or children of a schizophrenic patient have about a 10 per cent chance of developing the illness, and, if the patient being considered has one parent who is also schizophrenic, the frequency among the brothers and sisters is over 14 per cent. The incidence among less closely related blood relatives is lower than this, but is still much higher than in families hitherto free from the illness. When a patient marries another patient with the illness (not so very uncommon, as they may meet during sojourn in mental hospital), around 40 per cent of their children may be expected to develop schizophrenia.[198] The way schizophrenia runs in families does not in itself prove a genetic hereditary contribution to the cause of the disease, as might appear at first sight, because the parents who pass on their genes are also the people who bring up the children, and therefore might sow the seeds of the illness by their influence during that upbringing. However strong the family history of illness, upbringing as an environmental cause cannot be ruled out. Uncles and aunts share genes with the parents of the patient, so their liability to the family illness is explicable on genetic grounds; however, environmental theories can still be supported, because all will have been brought up by the grandparents in a way that may have predisposed all of them to develop schizophrenia later. Schizophrenic fathers pass on the illness to their children as frequently as do mothers with the condition,[198] a clear finding that does not support the theories about 'schizophrenogenic mothers' who are heard of so much more often than 'schizophrenogenic fathers'.

Many of the studies of family histories are now several decades old, and they were followed by the now classical research on twins and schizophrenia. Since identical twins are genetically identical, and fraternal (litter-mate, non-identical) twins are merely brothers or sisters born together, it was hoped that studies of the tendency of the different types of twins to develop schizophrenia would throw light on hereditary and environmental contributions to the genesis of the condition. Therefore, twins with schizophrenia were found and the other twin of each pair was traced and studied. Many results have been published, usually in the form of 'concordance' rates for schizophrenia, that is, in terms of the frequency with which schizophrenia is found in the twin brothers or sisters of the patients. In his review in 1978, Shields[198] discussed 11 studies of the identical and non-identical co-twins of over 1300 schizophrenics from seven countries, and ten of these comparisons showed a higher concordance rate among the identical twins. His careful analysis of the figures suggests that for

a best estimate of the average morbid risk for twins of schizophrenics, it would probably be wisest to rely on the recent studies. Rates of approximately 50% for MZ (monozygotic, i.e.

identical) pairs and 17% for DZ (dizygotic, i.e. non-identical) pairs may not be far from the mark. ... The main point is that several methodologically careful, well documented population-based twin studies agree in finding that genetically identical pairs are very considerably more alike in respect of schizophrenia than genetically dissimilar pairs, and that the difference is unlikely, to any appreciable extent, to be due to sampling or diagnostic bias or to the greater environmental similarity of the MZ pairs. They confirm that the genes make a difference.

This is strong evidence that genetic factors are very important, but a doubt still remains. Identical twins are brought up even more similarly than non-identical twins: they tend to be dressed more similarly, treated more similarly and experience more confusion and remarks by other people to the effect that they are virtually indistinguishable. Therefore, it is possible, and indeed plausible, that this extreme similarity of upbringing might induce high concordance rates for later experiences, including schizophrenia.

Put another way, the finding that about half of the identical twin pairs studied were *not* concordant for schizophrenia is incontrovertible evidence that it is not a purely hereditary illness. If it were so, as is, for example, haemophilia or red-green colour blindness, then in *all* the identical twin pairs where one was schizophrenic so too would the other be (although allowance would have to be made for a time factor: the other twin's illness might be latent and become noticeable later).

More crucial tests of the genetic hypothesis have been sought by studying situations in which the separate contributions to the make-up of the patient by heredity and upbringing could be distinguished. This can be done by examining the incidence of schizophrenia in identical twins brought up apart, and in adoption studies where information is available on both the original biological parents and the adoptive ones.

Identical twins are not often brought up apart, and in many of the reports they were brought up by relatives or in conditions where the styles of the two families could not be clearly distinguished. Nevertheless, as Shields points out, in about two-thirds of the 26 or 27 pairs reported by the time of his review, both twins had schizophrenia or a virtually indistinguishable disorder, which is a striking finding in favour of a very strong genetic influence on the illness.

In the first of the major adoption studies, carried out in the state of Oregon, Heston studied the children of schizophrenic mothers,[74] adopted immediately after birth when the mothers, presumably severe indubitable schizophrenics, remained in the mental hospital. He compared the results with those of children born of mentally healthy mothers and adopted at the same time. Of 50 control children, none was diagnosed as schizophrenic by the time of follow-up at the average age of 36, although seven had neurosis and disorders of personality. Of the 47 children of chronic schizophrenic mothers, five were schizophrenic, four mentally handicapped, 13 neurotic and nine had severe disorders of personality. So schizophrenia only occurred when there was a genetic connection with a schizophrenic mother, who played no part at all in bringing up the child. This shows that the high frequency of schizophrenia in the children of patients (about 10 per cent) is not caused by upbringing, but must be transmitted in the genes. However, the results are *not* specific for schizophrenia, and schizophrenic parentage appears to predispose to a range of psychiatric disorders.

The fact that cases of schizophrenia occurred only among the true children of schizophrenic patients, although striking, tends to obscure the other very interesting findings of Heston's study. Severe disorders of personality, neurosis and mental handicap were common in the experimental group, as already mentioned, as were also excessive drinking and some other objectively recorded indices of psychiatric disorder such as psychiatric or behavioural discharges from the Armed Forces (eight in the experimental group and one among the controls). Heston thought that the experimental subjects who were not psychiatrically disturbed were successful, and, in fact, unusually colourful and creative in their lives. Only among them were found the musically able and the people with unusually strong religious convictions. Overall, Heston concluded that, 'Within the experimental group there was much more variability of personality and behaviour in all social dimensions.' I shall return to this point and its possible meaning in Chapter 9.

The other adoption studies have been carried out in Denmark with Danish and American psychiatrists making joint diagnoses.[229] Of 69 children of schizophrenics who had been adopted and brought up away from their original parents, 19 per cent were probable or definite schizophrenics, while in a control series of adopted children of non-schizophrenics there was a 10 per cent incidence of schizophrenia – a high figure, and difficult to reconcile with the results from other series of adopted children. Tracing the genetic link in the opposite direction, from children to parents, Kety[104] counted how many of the biological and adoptive parents of adopted people diagnosed as schizophrenic, themselves suffered from the illness. He found that the biological parents of the schizophrenics included 12 per cent schizophrenic patients, and the adoptive parents 1.6 per cent, so that, again, high rates of the illness were found among those linked genetically, and not among those associated by upbringing.

Even if the results of the studies on twins and family history had been equivocal, and were only suggestive evidence for the importance of heredity in the transmission of schizophrenia from one generation to the next, the adoption studies make it clear that some genetic loading for schizophrenia must now be accepted as a cause. However, the actual mechanism remains unknown, and the existence of an important role for environmental influences in the illness is equally certain. Such a conclusion, after massive polemics and painstaking research, surprises few biologists and doctors, for one thing that has long been clear is that the causes of schizophrenia would be found to be multiple and complex, and were unlikely to exclude either genetic or environmental factors.

A great deal of thought has gone into attempts to work out a precise genetic mechanism for the transmission of schizophrenia, whether it be by multiple genes determining the trait (as is probably the case with the inheritance of height), or by a dominant gene that is only activated to cause expression of the illness in a proportion of the people in whom it is present. The theories have been complex because the figures do not fit any of the usual Mendelian patterns without *ad hoc* manipulation.[198]

I shall not discuss the theories here because it does not seem fruitful to do so while they remain unconvincing. However Edwards[47] has pointed out that, 'Genes of high specificity have not been shown to be either necessary or sufficient to cause the development of any common disease.' (There are a few exceptions, and the emphasis is on 'common'. Rare diseases can certainly be purely genetically determined, as is, for example, Huntington's chorea in psychiatry, but schizophrenia in this context is a common disease.) I agree with Shields, who, when discussing this,[198] says that 'Edwards' generalisation holds true for all the behavioural disorders in the sense that no specific genetic theory in regard to any of them has been clearly established.'

Biochemistry

The conviction that the cause of schizophrenia will turn out to be a biochemical disturbance of the brain is deep in modern psychiatry. This concept of the illness goes back to Kraepelin and Bleuler in the late 19th and early 20th centuries.[14,105] To these psychiatrists and most of their colleagues, the condition was like an illness disturbing the function of the brain, perhaps akin to the effects on behaviour of poisoning with lead or coal gas, drunkenness or low blood sugar. The psychiatrists were doctors, accustomed to seeing patients with disturbed behaviour caused by these chemical changes or intoxications, and naturally suspected that the causes of mental illness might turn out to be very subtle cerebral disturbances.

This conviction has persisted, and has been supported from time to time by new expectations of actually finding a biochemical cause, although disappointment has always followed. The evidence for a major role of heredity in the transmission of schizophrenia is itself proof that a biochemical mechanism is involved, for all that is passed on are the genes – DNA molecules in the genetic code – and at the most fundamental biological level, this means a chemical structure encoding instructions for the future individual.

In addition, there are many illnesses that are known to be due to inborn defects of metabolism, and that handicap mental function by the accumulation of internally produced chemicals: the most common example of these is phenylketonuria. Such illnesses usually handicap people severely from birth, whereas the widespread disturbances of mental function typical of schizophrenia do not begin until after childhood and sometimes occur quite late in adult life. However, in the case of Huntington's chorea, a strictly hereditary disease, the occurrence of which is determined by whether or not the individual carries the Mendelian dominant gene specific to the illness, there are usually no signs of the disease before the patient reaches middle age. The condition probably arises from a disorder of the metabolism of the brain neurotransmitter, gamma-aminobutyric acid. In Huntington's chorea, apart from troublesome involuntary movements, the resulting mental illness is a dementia, primarily with loss of memory and intellectual functions, and thus most unlike schizophrenia. Nevertheless, the mere existence of the illness offers some hope to biochemical researchers that they may one day be able to throw some light on schizophrenia.

From the 1950s onwards, further hope that biochemical causes would be found came from the interest in the hallucinogenic chemicals: mescaline; the constituents of the various sacred mushrooms; and the synthetically produced lysergic acid diethylamide, LSD. In addition to the wonder known to all of us that a few drops of alcohol can alter our state of mind, affecting mood, concentration and judgment, came the knowledge that only a few millionths of a gram of LSD can utterly change perceptions and induce hallucinations. Despite early exaggerated claims, there are many differences between the experiences induced by LSD and those of schizophrenia, so that the former cannot be used as a close model of the latter. Yet it remains an astonishing fact that such extraordinary and subtle mental disturbances, of the greatest vividness and interest, very different from the experiences of the physically ill, poisoned, hypoglycaemic, tired, sedated or drunken mind, can be regularly produced by such minute traces of a single chemical. In view of this, the suggestion that schizophrenia may be due to another biochemical disturbance cannot be regarded as far-fetched, despite the failure of the many theories of the last few decades.

Schizophrenia has been attributed to vitamin deficiencies; virus disease; sensitivity to wheat protein, as found in coeliac disease; and allergies.[72] In the 'pink spot' theory of 1962, the illness was thought to be related to the presence of an amine in the urine;[59] however, this was later found to be a mixture of substances which, despite the first reports, could not be isolated regularly from the urine of schizophrenics. There has never been any shortage of these physical, chemical and biological theories of schizophrenia proposed by those determined to prove it a medical disease, in pursuit of a cause with an identifiable physical basis – a pursuit which has been mocked as the '[pathetic] search for the schizococcus' or causative organism. Nearly all of the theories are in disarray, moribund or maintained only by the tenacity of a lone supporter, and only the dopamine theory needs elaboration, as the one with the strongest basis at the present day.

The dopamine theory[90] suggests that in schizophrenia there is over-activity in the central nervous system in the pathways involving the neurotransmitter chemical dopamine. The evidence in favour of the theory is twofold: the effect of the drug amphetamine; and studies of the drugs that have been found to help in the treatment of schizophrenia.

Amphetamine, and the drug apomorphine which has some similar actions, exacerbate the illness in schizophrenic patients, and cause an odd form of stereotyped behaviour in laboratory animals, a disturbance of no clear psychological significance but which is prevented from occurring if the animals have been given doses of the drugs that relieve schizophrenia in human patients.

In large doses, as have been taken by many addicts[34] and by normal volunteers during the course of experiments, amphetamine frequently induces severe mental disturbances similar to schizophrenia. There are delusions, very often of being pursued and persecuted, and auditory hallucinations. There is often no insight that the experience is abnormal and not based on events in the real world, and the psychosis can be difficult to distinguish from true schizophrenia as seen in a patient who has not taken amphetamine. As amphetamine appears to release dopamine in the brain, and does not affect other neurotransmitter chemicals in the same way, the disturbance of dopamine in the brain could be the natural mechanism of schizophrenia.

Unfortunately, further observations on the amphetamine psychosis suggest that it is not as close a model of schizophrenia as was thought.

The amphetamine-takers are more often overactive, the schizophrenics typically withdrawn; the hallucinations experienced by drug abusers are usually visual, this type being less common although not rare in schizophrenia; typical bizarre disorders of the logic of normal thinking scarcely occur except in true schizophrenia; and the drug takers are sometimes confused and clouded in their state of consciousness, with poor grasp, judgment and appreciation of what is going on around them. In other words, the amphetamine psychosis has just as many resemblances to a toxic delirium, a physical disturbance of the brain, as to classical schizophrenia.

Probably some explanation involving both physical and psychological mechanisms will be found for the position of the amphetamine psychosis somewhere between a hallucinatory toxic delirium and schizophrenia. For example, the alerting action of the drug may be described in physical terms as changing the function of the parts of the cerebral cortex that compute and organise the meaning of those perceptions that are filtered and selected for attention in the mind. This action on the brain could make the subject more liable to hallucinations, which in the case of the schizophrenic are most easily understood psychologically, as deriving from a mental state of intense withdrawal and self-absorption. This self-absorption makes mental events, that is thoughts, more vivid and less closely checked with perceptions from the outside world. Confusion arises between inner fantasy and outer reality. The patient fails to distinguish thoughts from perceptions: he has hallucinations, hearing what he calls real voices, but they are in his inner ear alone, inaudible to others.

The other data which have been used to support the dopamine theory concern the drugs which have helped in the treatment of schizophrenia, and their possible mode of action. Many different drugs are regarded with good reason as valuable forms of treatment, but they are not all of closely related chemical structure. In fact, they belong to three groups: the phenothiazines (first introduced in the early 1950s), the thioxanthenes and the butyrophenones. The evidence that these drugs specifically relieve schizophrenic symptoms, as distinct from merely having a sedative action to relieve agitation and distress, varies; however, for many of the drugs, for example chlorpromazine and trifluoperazine of the phenothiazine group, the evidence is compelling, and based on numbers of scrupulously careful scientific trials in which the actions of the drugs were compared with that of a placebo.[81, 82, 129, 165] (In such 'blind' trials, half of the test group of patients are given the drug, and half the placebo, but who has received which is not revealed to the patient, doctor or researchers until after the course of treatment has been completed.)

The effectiveness of the drugs in the relief of acute symptoms of schizophrenia, and in reducing the likelihood of relapse in patients who continue to take them, is striking and important, even though the underlying illness is not cured but rather suppressed or made to remit temporarily. The importance of the drugs in our present context is that all of those with established reputations in the treatment of schizophrenia, despite different chemical structures, have been shown to act as antagonists at dopamine receptors in the brain, so reducing the activity of dopamine. In fact, the range of doses of the various drugs that are effective in the treatment of the illness correlates closely with the doses which have been shown by laboratory experiments on brain tissue to block dopamine receptors.[196]

Nevertheless, there are weaknesses in the dopamine theory of schizophrenia, and in particular it has not been shown that the dopamine pathways actually are overactive in schizophrenia. Biochemical studies of different parts of the brain continue, but even if important biochemical abnormalities were to be found exclusively in schizophrenia, the illness could not be viewed simply as a disorder of metabolism, primarily without psychological meaning. Such changes might be secondary results of a process that was originally psychological or social. Frightened people have tense muscles, but apprehension is not a muscular disease, and similar cautionary reflections must apply to the significance of physical changes in the brain in mentally ill patients.

Disorders of the brain

Certain forms of brain damage are known to increase the liability to schizophrenia,[40] or, at least, to illnesses extremely similar to schizophrenia and liable to be diagnosed as such unless the cerebral damage is regarded as the prime diagnosis (since schizophrenia is regarded by definition as a residual group of mysterious mental illnesses). For many forms of brain damage, as for instance after head injury, the evidence is controversial but appears to show that schizophrenia is slightly more likely to appear later in the same patient. Sometimes a biochemical disturbance comes first but then leaves the patient in a hallucinatory state in clear consciousness, similar to schizophrenia: this can occur after some years of severe alcoholism. In the case of Huntington's chorea, a pseudo-schizophrenic type of disturbance sometimes comes to notice before it is overtaken and submerged in the cerebrally caused dementia of the disease.

In the specific case of epilepsy, especially severe epilepsy over many years originating from sites of damage in the temporal lobe of the brain, there seems to be a particularly close connection, documented by Slater.[203] Patients with severe epilepsy are liable to develop (in addition to the often extraordinary sensations induced during the disturbed electrical patterns in the brain around the time of the fits) long-standing mental illnesses with delusions, hallucinations concerning meaningful noises and imaginary voices, and sometimes even disorders of the logic of thinking and symbolism typical of schizophrenia. At times, such patients are confused, clouded in their consciousness, and unable to think and remember clearly, the usual syndrome found in physically ill patients and in widespread disorder of the function of the brain. The interesting finding, however, is that at most times they do not resemble the physically ill: they experience a state of mind resembling mental illness. Moreover, Slater's research found that these patients were not known as aloof 'schizoid' personalities before the onset of epilepsy, and they did not have a raised incidence of schizophrenia amongst their blood relatives, so that they were not typical of ordinary schizophrenics.

This suggests that long-continued and severe disturbances of this nature (on the average the patients had suffered from epilepsy for 14 years) are liable to induce their own illnesses of schizophrenic type and not merely to precipitate, or bring forward, the onset of the illness in an already vulnerable person.

Here we seem to have come close to finding a cerebral cause of schizophrenia, but many questions remain unanswered. The illnesses are not all completely typical cases of schizophrenia, and the interesting ones with the classical syndrome are at the end of a spectrum; at the other end are, more typically, cases with delirium, confusion and dementia – the syndrome of ordinary cerebral disorder, which is not at all like schizophrenia. I shall return to this in discussing a formulation of the whole problem in Chapter 9.

Another question which cannot be answered yet is whether the mental changes are 'caused' by, or linked with, the epileptic disturbances and the accompanying experiences, or whether the underlying abnormality in the brain, which disturbs the electrical pattern and provokes epileptic fits, also initiates processes leading to the long-lasting mental changes.

In either of these two cases, it is possible to suggest how some of the schizophrenic experiences could be produced. The temporal lobe contains the end-station and association networks for the pathway along which information from the ear is carried to the brain, coded as electrical impulses in the auditory nerve. The cortex of the temporal lobe is the key area in the mechanisms that attribute perceptual meaning to these impulses: our perception of sounds in the world around us is, in fact, mediated in the temporal lobe in unimaginably complex cerebral circuits. So it may be that disease in this part of the brain, in disturbing this function, could impair distinctions normally made there between auditory perceptions (e.g. I hear a voice in the outside world) and auditory imaginations (e.g. I know I am imagining someone talking). The patient might then report hearing someone really talking to him when in fact he is 'hearing [imaginary] voices'. He might or might not realise that he had lost the ability to distinguish between real and imaginary noises, depending on other aspects of the degree of his disturbance, cerebral or mental.

The experiences of patients during abnormal epileptic states can also help our understanding of the origins of other schizophrenic phenomena. Bizarre experiences can occur in epilepsy, including vivid hallucinations involving any of the five senses, in which the patient is severely withdrawn and may appear to be physically slowed and in a trance of self-absorption. It would be understandable for this to start an alienation from the outer world: an inward preoccupation with an increasing vividness of fantasy, and eventually a lasting inability to distinguish between the inner and outer worlds, even at times when the electrical patterns are normal and there is no epileptic disturbance in the brain. Delusions are best regarded, in these speculations as in others, as secondary phenomena concerned with making fragmentary and idiosyncratic sense of otherwise incomprehensible experiences, whether these are caused by the disturbance of temporal lobe mechanisms, as discussed above, or by the resulting epileptic discharges. Disturbance of thinking presumably goes hand in hand with alienation and withdrawal into private meanings – this is discussed later.

The research on possible genetic and physical causes of schizophrenia has yielded an impressive amount of evidence. It is hard evidence, gleaned by repeated criticism of earlier research, constantly improved by testing hypotheses and by discussion within the scientific tradition. Some findings are open to the criticism that they are unimportant physical correlates of those psychological events which have the true importance (as when minor biochemical abnormalities are found in depressed patients), but most are not, and the genetic findings in particular seem to have established a weighty physical contribution to the illness, in the sense that a blueprint for some aspects of the development of the individual is handed on in the genes. The outcome – how the person develops as a human being – obviously has the greatest psychological interest; but the original genetic basis for much of this appears to be well established, and is, in fact, scarcely disputed even by those concerned to emphasise how the patient's experience in life contributes to the development of schizophrenia.

We must now turn to the patient's psychology and his life.

7

Knowledge of causes (ii) Psychological causes

Psychological research

There have been many experiments designed to analyse scientifically the psychological disorders in schizophrenic patients, and I will now refer to some that may in the end throw light at least on the disability of schizophrenia and possibly on the original causes of it.

The hallucinations (experiences of perceptions in the absence of corresponding stimuli in the outside world: hearing voices in a silent room) and illusions (mistaking the nature of things in the outside world: seeing a shadow of a vase as a threatening man or hearing whispers in the sound of rustling leaves) typical of schizophrenia have inspired efforts to analyse wheher schizophrenics are abnormal in their capacity to deal with information from the outside world, and there have been some interesting findings, as discussed by Venables[226] in Wing's *Schizophrenia – towards a new synthesis.*[235] It seems that the patients are sensitive to overloading with more perceptions than they can handle or process, as if a filter present in all of us were defective in their case.

Of all the stimuli from the environment impinging on our sense organs, we normally perceive and attend to only a few, since there are essential mechanisms that suppress our conscious attention to peripheral sensations. Without these mechanisms, our attention would be continually distracted by fresh sensations, with no preservation of concentration on any object or theme. In schizophrenia, it has been found that there is a defect in this sensory filtering system, and the patient fails in the effort to select and control attention. This finding concurs with the accounts given by patients who report over-flooding by too many stimuli and say that they have the greatest difficulty in concentrating and avoiding distraction from moment to moment. People talking to schizophrenic patients notice that they often break off from a conversation and pay attention to a muffled noise outside the room, an aeroplane flying overhead, a piece of paper blowing down the road, a smell of cooking. A patient of McGhie and Chapman[147] described this: 'Everything seems to grip my attention although I am not particularly interested in anything. I am speaking to you just now but I can hear noises going on next door and in the corridor. I find it difficult to shut these out and it makes it more difficult for me to concentrate on what I am saying to you.' Psychiatrists find most of their schizophrenic patients in this state at some time. The self-imposed isolation of the schizophrenic may reflect an effort to reduce this disturbing experience, especially, as we shall see later, in relation to reducing social stimulation by other people.

McGhie and Chapman quote another patient, who gave his explanation for behaving like a statue, still and silent:[147] 'I don't like moving fast . . . If I carried on I wouldn't be aware of things as they really are. I would just be aware of the sound and the noise and the movements. Everything would be a jumbled mass. I have found that I can stop this by going completely still and motionless.'

Another finding that confirms what would be expected from the behaviour of the patients is the difficulty that schizophrenics have, in comparison with normal people, in detecting visual or auditory stimuli against a 'noisy' confusing background. In addition, defects in the vestibular organs of balance in the inner ear have often been found in schizophrenia, the patients being less liable to rotational giddiness but prone to spontaneous feelings of difficulty in orientating themselves in the world.[147]

Another phenomenon close to the enigmatic mind–brain boundary, arousal or vigilance and its psychological and bodily accompaniments, has thrown light on the problem of schizophrenia.[147] The aroused state represents the very alert, vigilant, tense, poised-for-action end of the range of states of alertness that runs from this state through less vigilant wakefulness and then, successively, peaceful inattention, drowsiness, sleepiness and deep sleep. There are corresponding physiological changes that can be used as measures of arousal – such as muscular tension, heart rate and measures of traces of sweating in the skin – which are high at the alert end of the range. Levels of arousal are high in anxious, worrying and tense people, but, less predictably, they are also usually high in schizophrenics, who frequently do not seem to be anxious in the same way. Moreover, the levels of arousal are particularly high in the withdrawn, chronic patients who at first sight appear to be apathetic and sluggish, as if far from vigilant. This important finding[227] needs further elucidation: it could be that the patients' state represents an attempt to protect themselves from the high arousal or extreme anxiety brought about by an overwhelming barrage of stimuli from outside, and from the body as well. The protection, the warding off of the stimuli, takes the form of slowing of the body, and curtailment of mental functions such as attention to the environment.

It is interesting to speculate whether these findings throw any light on the creativity of eccentric people and those called 'schizoid'. ('Schizoid' is used to describe a variety of aloof, remote person. The term is fully defined in Chapter 9.) There are accounts of some of the great creators in the arts and sciences being in withdrawn and quiet states for long periods, when they were, in fact, rapt in the deepest concentration, before they hit upon new ideas. Perhaps, as suggested by Lehmann,[130] schizoid people are highly sensitive to sensory stimuli, and are bombarded by them more richly than individuals of different make-up (whether the differences are genetic or environmental in origin, or, almost certainly, both). Then, if they are able to sort out, think about and act upon this richness of experience while protecting themselves from being submerged, they will be at an advantage in producing original creative work; however, those of a different mental capacity might become overwhelmed, and succumb to disintegration associated with abnormal distractibility, inability to distinguish between inner and outer experiences, and idiosyncratic styles of thinking. They might, in fact, become schizophrenic.

Furthermore, an article by Hasenfus and Magaro[70] points out that some tests of schizophrenic 'abnormality' and 'disability', such as highly unusual ways of classifying and sorting objects and ideas, are virtually the same as some tests used to select creative normal people.

This speculation about the affinity of schizophrenia and creativity provides one way of understanding how there might be a biological advantage to the species in the occurrence of schizophrenia, a condition in itself disabling and a handicap to fertility through the discouragement of marriage and having children. These biologically disadvantageous factors would tend to breed out the hereditary factors for the illness in the long course of evolution unless there were compensatory advantages, less obvious, in some aspect of the schizoid constitution or schizophrenic condition. This advantage might be the unusual creativity of some schizoid individuals – they might be socially favoured, slightly advantaged in breeding, and thus pass on in plentiful measure the genes involved in the transmission of schizophrenia. Whether this is so is not known, but it agrees with Heston's findings,[74] mentioned in the previous chapter, that among the children of schizophrenics adopted into other families who did not become mentally ill there were unusually colourful and creative people.

Schizophrenia itself usually cripples creativity in those who were successfully productive before its onset, and no misguided romantic views on the insanity of genius should allow us to forget this. The most productive and successful of all creative people may have been larger than life but were very sane: Shakespeare, Goethe, Dickens, Michelangelo, Rubens, Mozart, Napoleon. Neurotic symptoms and instabilities are common enough among the supremely creative, but schizophrenia is not. However, the possibility is that the schizoid state of personality, treading a narrow path between 'normality' and schizophrenia, can be an advantage in at least this one aspect of life.

In *The dynamics of creation*,[210] Storr explains why creative activity is a particularly appropriate way for the schizoid individual to express himself. The reasons are that creation is solitary, all interaction with other people being on his own terms; that it plays into fantasies of omnipotence harboured by such touchy aloof people; that creation as a way of life emphasises the importance of the inner world and its power to influence the outer, in works of art or the ideas of science, for instance; 'that certain kinds of creativity are peculiarly apt for overcoming the sense of arbitrary unpredictability' felt by solitary individuals with difficulties in personal relationships; and that 'creative activity can undoubtedly act as a defence against the threat which overhangs the schizoid person of finding the world meaningless'. Storr describes Newton and Einstein as particularly vivid examples of 'how schizoid detachment can be put to creative use'.

Theories of communication in the family

In contrast to the European tradition, strong in Germany, Scandinavia and Britain, which has considered schizophrenia as clearly an illness, probably of physical origin, the speculation in America has taken different lines. American institutions for most of the patients – the state hospitals – may have differed little from the asylums in Europe, but the predominant philosophy was, at least until recently, psychoanalytical – a psychological philosophy less interested in diagnosis and illness-entities. This meant that there was more concern with the family origins of the patients and with the style of communication within their families. The earlier view of all psychiatric illnesses, including schizophrenia, as forms of adaptation of the developing individual to abnormal situations led, in the 1950s and thereafter, to the theory that peculiar styles of communication are to be found in the families of schizophrenic patients. These styles of communication were then assumed, in a big jump of speculation, to have caused the illness, a very different matter.

The American theories of Lidz,[136] Wynne[242] and of Bateson and his colleagues[10] have been influential in psychiatry and in the world at large, and the theories on this side of the Atlantic, espoused in such compelling writing as Laing's *The divided self*[110] and later books, have captured the imagination of all who read them, especially, it can be noted, those readers who do not actually see and treat schizophrenic patients. The theorists certainly know the patients, but their theories nevertheless run far ahead of the evidence in support of them. Laing's writings in particular are not merely an advocacy of a theory of the origin and way of understanding schizophrenia, but also a romantic and rhetorical crusade on behalf of the victims and even against the sane world.[52, 135]

In Bateson's theory,[10] it is suggested that schizophrenic ways of thinking and behaving may be patterns of communication – not to be thought of as illnesses of the mind – understandable as responses to a family life full of communications in 'double-binds'. It is implied in all these family theories that the model case being considered is that of the young schizophrenic patient living with his parents. Often the parent quoted in examples of double-bind communication is the mother, the patient being her son, and the 'schizophrenogenic mother' driving her son mad is part of the received wisdom of our times, despite the lack of evidence for it and the approximately equal number of male and female schizophrenics. There is comparative silence among family theorists about the development of schizophrenia in middle age, in people living alone, in married people living with their spouse, and in the elderly and deaf.

In the double-bind, the parent is said to issue ambiguous instructions repeatedly, but they cannot be obeyed because at the same time they are contradicted by other instructions, in a different mode of communication. Thus, in one famous example, the mother tells her son to be close to her, hug her and feel at ease in physical contact, while she stiffens and implicitly repels such approaches by bodily signals. The victim may be exhorted to grow up and bring his mother happiness by getting married, while all efforts at independence are subtly undermined and sabotaged.

It is further said that the victim is trapped by being forbidden to merely go away and escape from the binding situation, and, especially in Laing's theories, which are in part similar to Bateson's, that an exquisite part of the confusion is the denial that there is any confusion or any injunction against leaving the situation. There is, in fact, a rule that says that one must not comment that there are rules, nor must one comment on this rule (or even recognise its existence) and so on, in infinite regress. Thus, in Laing's *Knots*,[124] from the patient's point of view:

They are playing a game. They are playing at not playing a game. If I show them I see they are, I shall break the rule and they will punish me. I must play their game, of not seeing I see the game.

The rule that one must not realise that there are hidden rules could be what is referred to in another of Laing's knots:[125]

> There is something I don't know
> that I am supposed to know.
> I don't know *what* it is I don't know,
> and yet am supposed to know,
> And I feel I look stupid
> If I seem both not to know it
> and not know *what* it is I don't know.
> Therefore I pretend I know it
> This is nerve-racking
> since I don't know what I must pretend to know.
> Therefore I pretend to know everything. . . .

The theory that, simply, a double-bind upbringing drives you mad, causing schizophrenia, has made sense at first sight to countless general readers, to young people identifying with the tormented children of incomprehensible members of the older generation, to those who could never understand how all the world except psychiatrists knows that people are driven mad for understandable reasons and not just by heredity and cerebral chemistry, and finally to many psychiatrists who have met the parents of schizophrenic adolescents and young adults and found them, in the now familiar term, 'mystifying'. The trouble is that the theory does not stand up so well to closer scrutiny. Double-binds, strictly defined by Bateson and his colleagues, are hard to identify in practice, and it has not yet been shown that they can be detected reliably and in an unbiased way. Furthermore, negative results have been obtained in an experiment to test whether double-binds are more common in the letters of the parents of schizophrenics to their children than in those of parents of normal offspring. (See also the discussion by Leff.[127]) Double-binds doubtless occur in many families, but they have *not* been shown to be specific to those of schizophrenics, despite the appeal of the concept of mystification with no escape. More research should be done on this subject.

Another theory of the family origins of schizophrenia that has been more psychoanalytically orientated is that of Lidz and his colleagues.[136] Very intensive study of the families of a small number of schizophrenic patients led Lidz to describe distorted styles of family structure and function, and to suggest that these styles had, while they were operative in the patient's childhood, *caused* the schizophrenic type of behaviour, which is again in this theory seen as a behavioural response to a family situation. The parents' marriages were said to be 'skewed' by the domination of the mother, whose often highly unusual and odd way of communicating became accepted in the family, covering underlying conflict; or 'schismatic', with more obvious conflict between emotionally separate parents, and complex involvement of the child in the conflict. The involvement of the children is thought to be stressful and mystifying for them; boundaries between people, between sex roles and between generations are more blurred than in most families; and the children who become schizophrenic patients fall into distorted perception, thinking and behaviour in response, albeit inappropriate response, to an alarmingly disturbed family situation.

It is Lidz' belief that,[137] 'Schizophrenic reactions are a type of withdrawal from social interaction, and the thought disorder is a specifically schizophrenic means of withdrawal,' and he further summarises: 'The schizophrenic patient escapes from irreconcilable dilemmas and unbearable hopelessness by breaking through these confines [i.e. the meanings and logic of his culture] to find some living space by using his own idiosyncratic meanings and reasoning, but in so doing impairs his ego functioning and ability to collaborate with others.'

Leff[127] examined the scientific status of the experiments that have provided the evidence on which the theory has been based, and found that, 'Where abnormalities of the kind described by Lidz have been identified in the families of schizophrenic patients, identical abnormalities have also appeared in control groups of families containing a member suffering from some other, or no psychiatric condition. Hence what Lidz and his group have derived from their uncontrolled in-depth investigation of this handful of families is not specific to schizophrenia.'

Another theory based on study of the families of schizophrenic patients is that of Wynne and Singer.[202] They also identified a peculiar style of life, this time called 'pseudomutuality', which, while appearing harmonious to those outside the family, in fact harbours deep gulfs between members, and irrational distorted modes of communication that fragment the thinking of that member of the family who becomes schizophrenic. Wynne and Singer tested the theory very carefully, studying samples of speech given by subjects talking about what they saw in the inkblots of the Rorschach test, and thus not about family problems and mental illness. The research workers found that, after training themselves, they could usually tell by listening to recordings of the discussion whether the participants were parents of schizophrenics, of neurotic patients or of healthy people.

This result, published in 1966,[201] was very important, but the scientific tradition required that its reproducibility be tested by another team. This was carried out by Hirsch and Leff[80] with English patients and their parents, after they had trained themselves to use Wynne and Singer's methods exactly. Their results were much less significant than those of the Americans, with a good deal of overlap in the degrees of abnormal communication scored by the parents of schizophrenics and by those of neurotic children. After analysis only one abnormality was left to be explained: the fathers of schizophrenic children tended to talk more than other fathers. Thus, the Wynne and Singer theory of specific peculiarities of communication in the parents of schizophrenics was not supported: the observed abnormalities doubtless occur, but in many unhappy families. As often happens, the original researchers had probably, without realising it, collected a biased sample of peculiarly communicating families, with the spotlight especially on a few with a schizophrenic member.

This process of generalising from a few families thought to be typical probably occurred also in the history of the concept of the 'schizophrenogenic mother', common currency of partially informed discourse on psychiatry, but based only on the clinical impressions of a few psychotherapists working with a few families. The term was coined around 1948 by Fromm-Reichmann,[60] and has survived since in descriptions of 'typical' mothers of young schizophrenics as being domineering, cold, distant and yet insensitively intrusive. The term blames some very unhappy people, and this is cruel whether it is true or untrue, and unjust if it is untrue. Yet the concept is espoused by people who criticise the usual psychiatric approach for being rejecting and cruel to the patients by, it is alleged, invalidating what they say by calling it insane.

The term's influence has descended via Bateson's double-binding parents, Lidz's maritally skewed and schismatic parents, and Wynne and Singer's pseudomutual families, with an offshoot to Kanner's[101] alleged 'refrigerator' parents of autistic children, to Laing's[126] parents who conspire to drive their children mad by mystifying them. The move to raise the status of the patient and lower that of the parents has swung with some authors, like a pendulum, to the opposite extreme from any earlier insensitivity to the claims of patients and reluctance to take seriously what they say. I agree with Siegler and Osmond[199] that Laing nowhere in *The politics of experience* or in any of his other books 'shows the slightest concern for the experiences of the other members of the family. He simply uses the information provided by the family interaction model to reinforce his argument that the schizo-phrenic patient has been driven mad by his family . . .'

Arieti, author of treatises on schizophrenia from a largely psycho-analytic point of view, and doyen of American writers on the subject,

has even admitted that parents have been unjustly called schizophrenogenic in many instances. In the 1974 edition of his *Interpretation of
schizophrenia*[3] (the first edition of which was in 1955), he writes that
he has concluded that only 20 per cent, or at the most 25 per cent, of
mothers are classical schizophrenogenic people. 'Therapists, including
myself, have believed what the patients told us. Inasmuch as a considerable percentage of mothers have proved to be just as they were
described by the patient, we have considered this percentage as typical
and have made an unwarranted generalisation that includes all the
mothers of schizophrenics.' Moreover, Lidz, too, while still espousing
the view that the family atmosphere induces schizophrenia, has in the
climate of recent times, when it has become fashionable to blame the
parents, specifically said that he does not believe 'that such torsions
exerted upon the patient's rationality have the purposeful malevolence
that these investigators seem to imply'.[138]

In Switzerland, Manfred Bleuler,[15] who has an unrivalled long-term
and close knowledge of nearly all the schizophrenic patients in one
mental hospital, and a lifetime's reflection on the condition, has
criticised the concept of the schizophrenogenic mother, because the
description is, in fact, not at all specific to the families of schizophrenics. Hirsch and Leff in 1975,[80] in their 100-page critical review
of the evidence on the abnormalities of the parents of schizophrenics,
write in similar vein of the '. . . concept of the cold, aloof, hostile
schizophrenogenic mother, for which, surprisingly in view of its
popularity, we could not find any reliable supporting evidence'.

Laing, in *The divided self*,[111] trying to make schizoid and schizophrenic persons comprehensible, writes that: 'Specifically, no attempt
is made to present a comprehensive theory of schizophrenia.' Nevertheless, an outline theory is discernible in that book, in *Sanity,
madness and the family*[126] written by Laing with Esterson, and in *The
politics of experience*[118] Laing says that, 'No attempt is made to
explore constitutional and organic aspects'[112] but this is clearly because
the theory is one of interpersonal and familial processes, as well as
wider issues of the sanity, or alienation, of society at large and the
people in it. 'Disease' is rejected because 'if we look at his actions as
"signs" of a "disease", we are already imposing our categories of
thought on to the patient',[113] and Laing suggests that, 'Sanity or
psychosis is tested by the degree of conjunction or disjunction
between two persons where one is sane by common consent.'[113]

'Schizophrenia', or rather 'the experience and behaviour that gets
labelled schizophrenic' (for it is Laing's concern to show that there is
no illness but there is certainly labelling), is, he asserts, 'without
exception . . . a special strategy that a person invents in order to live
in an unlivable situation. He cannot make a move, or make no move,

without being beset by contradictory and paradoxical pressures and demands, pushes and pulls, both internally, from himself, and externally from those around him'[121] (compare Bateson's double-bind). Mystifying family interactions are described vividly in these books and in *The leaves of spring* by Esterson,[50] which continues the account of one of the families in *Sanity, madness and the family.*[126]

These interactions seem to be regarded as possibly the origin of the schizoid condition and certainly as contributing to failure to recover from a schizophrenic episode. Laing quotes, 'with substantial agreement', the question posed by Bateson of whether those who fail to recover 'encounter circumstances either in family life or in institutional care so grossly maladaptive that even the richest and best organised hallucinatory experience cannot save them'.[121]

All Laing's readers have felt that the family and society are being blamed, but, in the case of the family at least, he does at one point moderate the charge of a deliberate intention to drive the patient mad. He says:[121]

The untenable position, the can't win double-bind, the situation of checkmate is by definition *not obvious* to the protagonists. Very seldom is it a question of contrived, deliberate, cynical lies, or a ruthless intention to drive someone crazy, although this occurs more commonly than is usually supposed. We have had parents tell us that they would rather their child was mad than he or she should realise the truth. Though even here, it is because they say that 'it is a mercy' that the person is 'out of his mind'.

Like the theories of the psychotherapists derived from their intimate knowledge of a small number of families, Laing's ideas are compelling: to laymen they sound as though they could well be true, and they offer a way in which schizophrenia and madness can be understood without the need for the technical theories of genetics and biochemistry offered by psychiatrists. Many psychiatrists, too, find that Laing is describing, with penetration and sensitivity, the families of patients whom they have met. However, unfortunately, this is not enough. Other questions have to be answered: Are other families like this too? Does the psychotherapist interested in the role of allegedly mystifying patients find what he expected to find? What is the state of the scientific evidence when it is reviewed?

Here it is necessary to cite Hirsch and Leff's summary of 'what has been established':[80] the parents of schizophrenics are more often psychiatrically disturbed than the parents of other children, thinking 'allusively', and living in very unhappy marriages; and the mothers are more often of schizoid personality themselves. The mothers also show more concern and protectiveness for the children than do other groups of mothers, and this was so before the children fell ill with schizophrenia (and therefore cannot be wholly a result of the child's disability). None of these findings is specific to the families of schizophrenics – all kinds of unhappy and disturbed relationships are found at times in other, 'normal' families. One can only agree with Hirsch and Leff's guess that the cause of schizophrenia is sure to be complex, and that the tortuous communications and intense relationships described with such care by the psychotherapists, and discussed above, are ingredients in some way not yet fully understood in the family environmental contribution to the cause of the condition. They write that, 'It seems likely that the popular theorists are describing ways of behaving which generate high emotion or overinvolvement. This is a form of stress which, according to the recent environment model [see below], is likely to precipitate florid schizophrenia in the vulnerable individual.'[80]

None of 'what has been established' disproves the hypothesis that the cause is truly hereditary, the genes often making the parents abnormal individuals, handicapped in relationships and marriage, prone to allusive thinking and other distorted modes of communication, while the children's illness could be determined by heredity and not by the parents' disturbance. This would account for the other established finding that 'the preschizophrenic child more frequently manifests ill-health or mild disability early in life than the normal child'. Such frailty in the children would explain the finding that the mothers are more protective towards them even before the onset of mental illness. Later, when the children manifest schizophrenic disability, some overconcern by the parents would be expected. Such overconcern is found in the families of all handicapped children, and is not specific to those of schizophrenics.

The eagerness to blame the parents for the illness, their responsibility being apparently confirmed, in less thoughtful quarters, by the observation that they are often odd, has ignored the possibility that the chain of cause and effect is the other way round – perhaps disturbed children disturb their parents. Even Searles,[194] an early proponent of the theory that people 'drive the other person crazy', was quite clear that this applied both up and down the generations, and described a mother who, in his opinion, 'showed the effects of yearslong exposure to an extremely poorly integrated psychotic person'.

No more is known about this likely possibility, which has been insufficiently studied, but there is excellent research and well founded knowledge on familial and social influences on the course of the illness, and on causes of relapse, if not yet on the original vulnerability and onset of disturbance.

Influences on the course of the illness

Schizophrenia as a description was born in the asylums of Europe, and depended on studies of the patients undergoing long periods in them. Kraepelin's[105] original description of the illness entailed almost inevitable chronic deterioration with very little chance of recovery, a pessimistic prognosis that has dominated psychiatric studies ever since. Observation of the chronic 'deteriorated' schizophrenics in the deprived conditions of the unchanging back wards of mental hospitals led to the supposition that the patients were so withdrawn as to be unresponsive to their environment. In practice, in this end-state, they were indeed largely unresponsive, but any assumption that they were not acutely sensitive to their surroundings has been shown to be quite wrong.

Making the environment more stimulating has been shown to improve the clinical state of the patients without any specific treatment of the disease. Barton[6] recounted how the patients became more responsive and lively when individual clothes and possessions were restored to them, in contrast with the bleak anonymous regimentation of the early regimes. Barton's study was anecdotal although detailed, but was confirmed by the studies of Wing and Brown, described in *Institutionalism and schizophrenia*.[237] They noted that the deterioration of the patients was worse under the more dreary hospital regimes, and when these were improved by the introduction of the open-door policy, more visitors, more individuality, and by providing the chance to do useful work, the patients improved in proportion to these measures. 'Signs of schizophrenia', such as withdrawal, apathy, and being nearly or completely mute, are, in fact, signs of the effects on untreated schizophrenia of a socially isolated and deprived situation. (This 'clinical poverty syndrome', investigated by Wing in a long series of research studies that are still continuing, is certainly not confined to institutions: it occurs in neglected schizophrenic patients at home, the cause again being the untreated disabilities of the condition, in a particular socially disabling environment. Some patients with severe disabilities spend as much time doing nothing staring into space when they are at home as they do when in a poor ward of a hospital.)

Clinical research has shown that relapse of schizophrenia leading to admission to hospital is often preceded by important events in the patient's life during the previous few weeks.[13] This applies even to events that could not possibly have been caused by his peculiar behaviour early in the relapse. Any important changes can have this effect, even exciting and stimulating ones, in contrast to the severe depressive process, which seems specifically to follow losses of people or precious ideals. Again, schizophrenics are found to be highly reactive to the events of life around them, and vulnerable to being upset by them, contrary to earlier assumptions (by which neurosis was thought to be reactive to stress, and psychosis, including schizophrenia, to be independent and constantly occurring in some remorseless, endogenous way).

When patients who have improved are discharged from hospital, the social environment to which they go has been found to affect how well they fare.[21] On average, they do better when living in emotionally neutral places like hostels than with their own relatives. Painstaking analysis of what goes on in the families after discharge, and comparisons of different families, have shown some details of the factors leading to relapse. The descriptions are simple and one-dimensional compared with the descriptions of the psychotherapists, but they are reliably established and clearly defined.[20,225]

Relapse of schizophrenia occurs particularly in families in which the parents or spouse criticise the patient when talking about him, not merely describing his behaviour as burdensome, but running him down as a person. Similarly, when the relatives are 'emotionally overinvolved' with the patient, as defined by psychiatrists on the basis of minute analysis of tape-recordings of interviews in the home, he will relapse more often. The amount of time that the patient and relatives spend together affects the fate of the patient, and, if the amount of face to face contact can be reduced, his prospects of remaining well in a critical but emotionally over-involved family improve. There has also been well-based research on the effect of the drugs used to treat schizophrenia, with the unsurprising but important result that, in emotionally disturbed homes, drugs and decreased contact with relatives confer protection on the patient against relapse.

Epidemiological research on social factors

I have been drawing back my viewpoint so as to survey ever wider fields. The genes and metabolism were my first objects of review, then came the brain, and then the psychology of the person. A look at family theories was concerned with what happens between the members of the small group, and now, at a further remove from the individual, I shall consider the research, carried out in the medical tradition, that has focused on the social data relevant to the cause of schizophrenia as diagnosed by psychiatrists.

There have been many studies on the frequency of schizophrenia in different countries, and despite differences in the criteria by which schizophrenia is diagnosed, the figures do not vary very widely.

Cooper[36] reviewed the main results of the surveys of the prevalence of the illness, and in most countries found the prevalence rate to be between 2 and 4 per 1000 of the total population. The risk of a person developing the illness during his lifetime is just under 1 per cent in many Western countries, but is 1–3 per cent in the United States where, it is now known through the research described in Chapter 4, doctors diagnose schizophrenia by wider criteria than in most other countries.

'Age- and sex-specific rates', summarises Cooper,[36] 'as a rule, show peak incidence rates within the range 20–39 years, with a smaller secondary peak in the over-65 range. Typically onset is earlier in men, whereas women have higher rates in the older age-groups.' The differences between the rates in the two sexes have always been slight wherever they were recorded, and have not given rise to any interesting speculations.

In the case of other illnesses, variations in frequency in different countries have often suggested theories for their cause, but with schizophrenia the formulation of a theory is, as ever, rendered more difficult by the uncertainty of the figures and the different factors of bias involved. On the whole, the variations have been small, this constancy among very diverse cultures being quoted by many psychiatrists to support suggestions that the illness is mainly caused by a genetic predisposition found more or less equally in all races. A famous area of high incidence was found by Böök[17] in an isolated part of Swedish Lapland: the population was inbred with many marriages between cousins, and might have been loaded with schizoid people fairly well adapted to a life of scanty social contact, other personalities having left the area. Another famous example of a particular people with an unusual frequency of schizophrenia, in this case a low rate, were the Hutterites of Canada and the United States, who formed religious communities with great emphasis on piety and the eschewing of violence. Cooper[36] points out that this finding has not been confirmed by rates of hospital admission for schizophrenia, so the original reports may have been misleading.

Admission rates over time have been studied, particularly in America, where in some areas they have been available for over 100 years since the early days of asylum statistics in Massachusetts in 1840. Goldhamer and Marshall[65] found no change there between 1840 and 1940. If this is a valid result, it must mean either a very remarkable stability in the true incidence of the illness during a period of considerable social change, perhaps because the main factors in causing schizophrenia are independent of the environment (such as genetic predisposition), or that the rates of the illness were affected in different ways by different factors, which by chance approximately cancelled out. We do not know which is more likely, and we need good comparisons with other areas. In New York, by contrast, the incidence of schizophrenia seemed to have increased[149] in this century, but this may have been caused by a change in diagnostic habits by which schizophrenia has come to be more readily diagnosed by psychiatrists in New York than elsewhere, while other mental illnesses have been recognised correspondingly less.

Studies in many different countries of the frequency of schizophrenia by social class have always shown that it is notably more common in the lowest classes, at the bottom of society.[36]

There are two rival interpretations of this important piece of information: the first, that conditions in the lowest classes are particularly conducive to the development of schizophrenia; the second, that the illness and the preceding period drive the patients into a deterioration of their ability to manage life in society, so that they tend to drift downwards to the level of the unskilled. The evidence has tended to accumulate in favour of the 'downward drift' hypothesis. Certainly the differences are not accounted for by differential labelling in the classes, by which schizophrenics in the top social classes might be cushioned from the demands of life, protected by friends, relatives and unearned income from having to earn their living, and manage to be regarded as eccentrics at large rather than mentally ill patients requiring hospital treatment. The number of such patients who would be concealed and not come to the attention of epidemiologists would in any case be small.

When the origins and social class of the patients' parents and grandparents were studied, they were found to be normally distributed, so that the schizophrenics had tended to drift downwards into the bottom social class, where the epidemiologists found them, as they succumbed to the illness and failed to fulfil the potential of their earlier lives. Such people are often found in the deteriorated centres of the large cities, living alone in lodging houses and bedsitting rooms. The origins of the patients are crucial in disproving other theories: that social forces in the lower classes increase the rate of schizophrenia or that psychiatrists are more prone to diagnose schizophrenia as a label for deviant behaviour and inability to cope with life in these classes than in higher ones. Thus Arieti[4] comments on the higher rates of schizophrenia in northern, industrialised Italy as compared with those in the more backward traditional areas in the south of the country, after allowing for the different availability of hospitals and possibly different willingness to be identified for treatment in the two areas, and is convinced that the difference is real. He interprets the difference in an elaborate theory, put forward for its plausibility but with no supportive evidence, that the nature of industrial society makes schizophrenia more frequent. He argues that urbanisation dis-organises the traditional family, which in Naples and the south is still in the extended version found in societies before the industrial revolution.

The family, according to this theory, becomes less truly intimate as it becomes the nuclear family of parents and children under one roof. Fathers go out to work in remote jobs, away from their children, while mothers are robbed of their traditional housekeeping skills, becoming bored housewives who long for a career and are ambivalent about motherhood. It is harder for the children to spend time away from the nuclear family, whereas, in the traditional culture, forays out with father, uncles and elder brothers are easy and natural. The descrip-tion, fluent, unoriginal and unsupported, easily explains the apparent increased incidence of schizophrenia in modern life, which Arieti believed he had seen in Italy at least but, we saw, was not apparent in Massachusetts. Arieti used the theory as a vehicle for a savage attack on the family:[3] 'The nuclear family consists of a small number of people who live in little space, compete for room, for material and emotional possession, and are ridden by hostility and rivalry. The home is often deprived of educational, vocational and religious values. The nuclear family is frequently destructive not only for the children but for the parents, too.'

Many other authors have suggested that the concept of schizo-phrenia, and how it is diagnosed, have social origins that need examining in quite different ways from the medical research con-sidered in this chapter. Similar conclusions may be reached from different starting points: Arieti, a psychiatrist, and Scull,[190] a sociologist studying asylum statistics from the 19th century, came to similar conclusions about the effect of the industrial revolution in increasing the number of the insane sent to asylums. I shall look at these different points of view from traditions other than the medical one in the next chapter.

8

Odd men out

Research into social causes of schizophrenia has been psychiatric in basis, the diagnosis being used as the starting point to define the field of study. However, more radical questions have been asked by sociologists and others outside the medical tradition. Does 'mental illness' exist or is it only a metaphor used to give the medical profession power over the insane? How is schizophrenia diagnosed – and why? What is its place in society?

Scheff, in *Being mentally ill*, offers 'a sociological theory', although he admits that it is only an outline, not intended as a rejection of medical theories but to offer a provocative contrast to them. He says that he is not commenting on the causes of acute illness and its onset, but is offering a view on the chronic and relapsing condition. He constructs 'a theory of mental disorder in which psychiatric symptoms are considered to be labelled violations of social norms, and stable "mental illness" to be a social role'.[183]

Society sets many strict rules governing conduct, and they are no less powerful for being often unconsidered, taken for granted, implicit, or for 'going without saying'. There are narrow limits within which we must conduct ourselves with other people. We must not shout, we must not whisper, we must not stand too close nor too far away from someone we are talking to. Looking away from him too much is to be oddly withdrawn; looking directly at him can be bad manners if it is defined as staring. When the rules are broken, the behaviour is categorised in various ways as, for example, bad mannered, drunken, perverse or criminal. 'After exhausting these categories, however, there is always a residue of the most diverse kinds of violations, for which the culture provides no explicit label.' At this point Scheff's theory becomes vague, and refers to two examples: the norms of what is decent, and what is apprehended as real. Violations of the rules in these two areas are said to be residual rule-breaking, and include witchcraft, spirit possession and mental illness.

Decency seems out of place here, as it is largely included in good manners. The proposal that there is a residual unnamed category seems unsatisfactory, and unnecessarily so. An important category is unlikely to be unnamed, and of course it is not: we know that madness is recognised in most cultures, as discussed in Chapters 4 and 5, and there is no obvious need for it to be in a logically different category from crime and the other infractions of the rules of society.

Scheff offers no theory of the causes or origin of the original rule-breaking behaviour, but points out that it is probably far more common than is reflected by the cases that come to attention as problems.

If the person behaving outrageously or oddly is regarded as a problem by his family or wider social group, this labelling ('he must be mad') makes him henceforth deviant, according to the theory, a category depending not on the nature of the original behaviour but on the surrounding social response to it. He then adopts the social role of the mentally ill patient, and the psychiatrist examining him will find the symptoms and signs of psychosis. In the eyes of his family or the psychiatrist, deep thinking becomes unnatural withdrawal, working out possible conversations in his head becomes listening to hallucinatory voices, trying according to his lights to understand the meaning of existence becomes the 'pseudo-philosophical ruminations' of psychiatric textbooks. Socrates has been called schizophrenic for standing lost in thought in the cold,[243] and there are many famous extraordinary men whom psychiatrists have tried to diagnose, labelling their actions as abnormal. St Paul on the road to Damascus and George Fox the Quaker have often been regarded as in the same category as the schizophrenics.

Accounts critical of psychiatry often give examples of the different points of view: the patient thinking and trying to make sense of his problem; his family and the police agreeing on mental abnormality and sending for psychiatrists, who are then cast in the role of, at best, insensitive pigeon-holers and categorisers of the vagaries of their fellow men, when they should be listening and understanding. At worst, they are seen as acting like policemen to lock away society's awkward eccentrics who break rules and implicitly criticise the system. Psychiatrists are certainly pilloried for this by Szasz in *The manufacture of madness*,[214] Goffman in *Asylums*[63] and Laing in *The divided self*.[110]

Scheff supports his theory 'that most chronic mental illness is at least in part a social role, and that the societal reaction is usually the most important determinant of entry into that role'[183] by reporting studies of procedures for examination before commitment to hospital in an American state, in which the doctors appeared to be acting scandalously rapidly, prejudging the patients' insanity in a few minutes. The evidence, although said to be from a state 'noted for its progressive psychiatric practices',[184] has not impressed people in this country, where the procedures under the Mental Health Act of 1959 were different and not much criticized until the last five years.

Szasz in *The myth of mental illness*[212] and *The manufacture of madness*[214] also claims that there is no mental illness beyond a crude analogy with physical illness, the 'symptoms' being, in fact, personal tactics and social responses. His polemic is very wide-ranging and, although it is loosely and erratically argued, has been very influential, especially among those who enjoyed his attack on the conventional psychiatric point of view. They believed, because they wanted to, that he was the innocent child telling the crowd that the Emperor of what he calls 'Institutional Psychiatry' has no clothes – no mental illness. His views, like those of Laing, to be mentioned shortly, have been espoused particularly by those, whether in the humanities or sociology, who are able to treat psychiatry as an armchair subject of theoretical disputation, without actually meeting patients and under-taking their treatment.

Szasz argues that hysteria was redefined as an illness by Charcot and Freud in the 19th century, whereas it was and is still, in reality, an elaborate game of mimicking physical illness, very near indeed to ordinary malingering. In this Szasz is clearly making a relevant point about the unsatisfactory concept of hysteria as an illness or disability. However, he is extrapolating outrageously when, in a mere aside in parentheses, he extends his theory on hysteria to psychiatry as a whole: '(. . . we may dispense with considerations of the physico-chemical causes or mechanisms of hysteria (and of other mental illnesses too), since there is neither observational evidence nor logical need for them) . . . So-called mental illnesses share only a single significant characteristic with bodily diseases: the sufferer or "sick person" is more or less disabled from performing certain activities. The two differ in that mental illnesses can be understood only if they are viewed as occurrences that do not merely happen to a person but rather are brought on by him (perhaps unconsciously), and hence may be of some value to him. This assumption is not necessary – indeed, it is insupportable – in the typical cases of bodily illness.'[213]

The argument proceeds in *The manufacture of madness*[214] with lurid comparisons of compulsory psychiatric admission to hospital with the persecution of witches by the Inquisition. Witchcraft was a myth, so is mental illness; patients also are persecuted. In each case some people adopt the role expected of them and seem to confirm the myth. He suggests that psychiatrists in the employ of the state act as society's policemen in incarcerating the modern heretics who say and do what they should not. However, his examples are oddly chosen: two chapters are devoted to homosexuality, on which subject British psychiatrists at least have never been accused of victimisation. Much of Szasz's polemic must be rooted in backward American psychiatry up to the 1960s, for certainty what he attacks cannot be recognised in Britain. For example, he quotes the proportion of voluntary psychiatric patients in the United States as 10 per cent.[215] The present British figure is nine times higher than this, 89 per cent of patients being admitted as completely free citizens.[41]

For Szasz, deviance, scapegoating, doctors' behaviour and the supposed persecution of victims which follows, are all illuminated at once in an almost fanatical tirade:

> Institutional Psychiatry is largely medical ceremony and magic. This explains why the labelling of persons – as mentally healthy or diseased – is so crucial a part of psychiatric practice. It constitutes the initial act of social validation and invalidation, pronounced by the high priest of modern scientific religion, the psychiatrist; it justifies the expulsion of the sacrificial scapegoat, the mental patient, from the community. . . . The principal social institutions involved in the theory and practice of psychiatric violence are the State, the family and the medical profession. The State authorizes the involuntary incarceration of 'dangerous' mental patients; and the medical profession, through psychiatry, administers the institution and supplies the necessary justifications for it.[215]

The medical profession was observed at work in American mental hospitals by the extremely critical eye of Rosenhan's investigators in the famous account of *Being sane in insane places*.[177] Normal volunteers presented themselves to hospitals claiming to be hearing voices saying 'empty', 'hollow' and 'thud'. They were admitted, in nearly all instances, with a diagnosis of schizophrenia, and then ceased to mislead the staff: they merely observed the hospital's reaction to them. They reported that the 'patients' were so consistently assumed to be abnormal that the staff ignored simple friendly greetings, and interpreted innocuous behaviour as consistent with schizophrenia. A normal life history was reported among the staff as redolent of psychopathology, and the pseudopatient who was making notes was reported by the nurse as 'engaging in writing behaviour'. Rosenhan also points out the way in which the long-lasting stigma of mental illness is affixed to patients, in that the pseudopatients were diagnosed in their discharge summaries as 'schizophrenia – in remission', as opposed to 'cured', 'healthy' or 'sane'.

The experiment has been regarded as unfair by the professions, which it appears to put in a bad light. It is, of course, to be expected that doctors and nurses can be deceived by deliberate fraud, when normally they can assume cooperation from their patients, and an occasional malingerer can fool any hospital department. The fraud involved in the initial complaints has tempted the professions to cast doubt on the results of the research, so that, for example, in *Reasoning about madness,*[233] Professor Wing, on each occasion that he mentions the experiment, refers to the investigators' 'lies'. However, this is over-defensive, and I submit that the experiment is infuriating also because it is humiliating and trenchant. It suggests that, at 12 different mental hospitals, patients were admitted for an isolated symptom without any other sign of disturbance, that schizophrenia was diagnosed on inadequate criteria, that the condition of the inpatients was not reviewed critically, and that the atmosphere in the wards was indeed that of staff 'labelling' the patients as insane, and having their perception and interpretation of the patients unwittingly prejudiced towards insanity by the institution's policy of labelling.

There is no doubt that the experiment describes very poor and insensitive psychiatry, although it is wrong to generalise from this to psychiatry practised well; however, it also challenges us to beware of the power of labelling and to reduce it wherever professional staff work with patients. It vividly illustrates the 'medicalisation' of human problems and behaviour, so that the nurse in a ward sees not a man writing, but an insane patient with writing behaviour to be observed and reported to the doctors, in case it is a sign of the illness from which the patient is presumed to be suffering.

The same points were made more fully by Goffman in *Asylums,*[64] which anatomises the mental hospitals with a clear sociological worm's eye view. He is extremely sceptical of all psychiatric claims and consistently regards the patients as being in hospital for social rather than individual, medical reasons, even when he candidly admits that he could not suggest a better way of handling persons called mental patients. He says, 'Mental hospitals are not found in our society because supervisors, psychiatrists and attendants want jobs; mental hospitals are found because there is a market for them. If all the mental hospitals in a given region were emptied and closed down today, tomorrow relatives, police, and judges would raise a clamour for new ones, and these true clients of the mental hospital would demand an institution to satisfy their needs.'[64]

Similarly, in Laing's writing, illness is denied as far as possible (although he is forced to refer to schizophrenia, insanity and psychosis in his patients), and sanity is defined relatively rather than absolutely: 'I suggest therefore that sanity or psychosis is tested by the degree of conjunction or disjunction between two persons where the one is sane by common consent'.[113] Of a man split between a 'true self' and a 'false self', with many odd ideas, he writes: 'Such ideas and experiences tend to isolate a man from his fellows in our present Western culture and, unless they serve at the same time to draw him into a small group of similar "eccentrics", his isolation is greatly in danger of passing over into psychotic alienation.'[115]

On labelling the prospective patient as insane in his social surroundings, Laing says: 'In using the term schizophrenia, I am not referring to any condition that I suppose to be mental rather than physical, or to an illness, like pneumonia, but to a label that some people pin on other people under certain social circumstances. The "cause" of "schizophrenia" is to be found by the examination, not of the prospective diagnosee alone, but of the whole social context in which the psychiatric ceremonial is being conducted.'[120]

In particular, he believes that the incomprehensibility attributed to schizophrenia by many psychiatrists has been exaggerated, maintaining rather that the condition is full of cryptic messages, and has intention and purpose. Thus, he states (although earlier he had denied that he was presenting a theory of schizophrenia[112]): '*Without exception* the experience and behaviour that gets labelled schizophrenic is *a special strategy that a person invents in order to live in an unlivable situation*' (Laing's italics).[121] Vagueness of thinking is seen as a defensive smoke-screen in a family where all clear communications from the patient are criticised, while the other members talk in a mystifying way.

According to this way of thinking, the psychotic feeling that the body is under the influence of others is to be understood as a drastic development of the alienated schizoid's feeling that his individual existence lies in his inner self and that his body is operated by him only to comply with others. The sane experience that one's thoughts are not fully under one's control becomes the psychotic one that the thoughts are in fact controlled by others. It is not meaningless but a cryptic comment on the true situation, when a schizophrenic says that a witch is putting thoughts into his head, if it turns out, when the family are interviewed, that his mother does not let him think for himself and frequently says, 'You don't really think that; what you *really* think is . . .'.

Laing and others following the same course have argued that hallucinations and delusions, the hallmarks of insanity, often refer, albeit obliquely, to real events in the patient's life, especially with his parents in childhood. This is shown by Schatzman, using documentary evidence on the childhood of Daniel Paul Schreber, the judge whose severe schizophrenic illness, as recorded in his own memoirs, was studied by Freud[58,186] (see Ch. 5). As described earlier, Schreber's father was a doctor who published books on medical gymnastics and held remarkable views on discipline in the upbringing of children.

Schatzman was able to demonstrate parallels between the son's psychotic experiences and his father's teachings, which we must assume he put into practice with his own son.[182]

> The son experiences his thinking and all else about himself as under the alien surveillance of what he called the 'writing-down' system, having said that 'Books or other notes are kept in which for years have been written down all my thoughts, all my phrases, all my necessaries . . . I presume that the writing down is done by creatures given human shape on distant celestial bodies . . . but lacking all intelligence.'[182]

The father wrote that,

> In families . . . a quite effective means of education is a punishment board, which is to be stuck upon the wall of the children's room. Such a board would list the children's names and against them every committed misdeed; all ever so little signs of omission, all instances of insubordination, would be chalked up as a tick or by a remark.[182]

The son complained of miracles of heat and cold enacted against him daily; the father insisted on a regime of cold ablutions for children over the age of 6 months. The son felt that his eyes and eyelids were influenced and moved against his will by miracles from God; the father prescribed repeated visual exercises and treatment of the eyes with cold water. The son felt prevented by a malign influence from sitting or lying down in comfort; the father explained regimes to keep the spinal column straight by constant criticism of the child's posture ('Half resting in lying or wallowing positions should not be allowed: if children are awake they should be alert and hold themselves in straight active positions and be busy'). The son suffered the 'compression-of-the-chest miracle'; the father invented a clamp pressing against the collar bones and shoulders to prevent crooked posture, and said that it proved its worth time and again with his own children.[182]

The case is convincing that Schreber must have been remembering experiences in childhood, although he did not consciously refer them to his father. He feels the victim of 'soul murder', and at first suspects the psychiatrist. Only much later did it become clear to him that 'God Himself must have known of the plan, if indeed he was not the instigator, to commit soul murder on me.'[182]

However, these parallels and reminiscences do not prove that childhood experiences cause schizophrenia. They suggest only that once schizophrenia is present, the extraordinary experiences of the patient may refer obliquely to real events in childhood. Schatzman's argument is that there is no such illness as 'schizophrenia', but instead a persecuted childhood that results in a mystified patient who is considered by outsiders to be crazy. Schatzman has no theory to explain why Schreber does not fall ill until middle-age. He states the mystification theory of the causation of schizophrenia:

> Schreber retains memories of what his father did to him as a child; although part of his mind knows they are memories, 'he' does not . . . He is considered insane not only because of the quality of his experiences, but because he misconstrues their *mode*: he *remembers,* in some cases perfectly accurately, how his father treated him, but thinks he *perceives* events occurring in the present for which he imagines God, rays, little men, etc. are the agents . . . Schreber knows what he most needs to know, but does not know he knows it. When he calls his experiences 'miracles', he denies what he knows, denies he is denying anything, and denies there is anything to deny, *and* he denies those denials, too . . . It is as if Schreber is forbidden by a rule to see the role his father has played in his suffering, and is forbidden by another rule to see there is anything he does not see . . . Why did Schreber turn memories into miracles? My hypothesis is that he did because his father had forbidden him to see the truth about his past. His father had demanded that children love, honour and obey their parents . . . Schreber, in order to link his suffering with his father, would have had to consider his father's behaviour towards him as 'bad'. This, I infer, his father had forbidden him to do. He is unable, or unwilling, to violate his father's view of what his view of his father should be. Prohibited from seeing the true origin of his torments, he calls them miracles. Similarly, forbidden from remembering his father's punishment board as such, he re-experiences it as God's 'writing-down system'. As a result, he is considered crazy.[182]

A main concern of Schatzman, and also of Laing, has been to show that schizophrenic behaviour is not incomprehensible, as has often been claimed and used as a criterion by psychiatrists, and that it is not a mere by-product of brain disease (as Dr Weber, one of the doctors, says in his addendum to Schreber's memoirs, the 'miracles' are 'undoubtedly due to pathological processes of the brain'[188]).

Many people are baffled by the behaviour of persons seen as schizophrenic. I suggest that were they to meet in depth, individually and as a 'family', as I have, the persons composing the families of such persons, they might find them no less bewildering than the so-called psychotic offspring. It would, I expect, become easy to see that to be able to live in such families might require special, devious, and even bizarre strategies.[181]

There is a point of view that schizophrenia goes beyond a stratagem to survive in impossible families, and can be positive, even on occasion a healing process. In Laing's *The politics of experience,* it becomes a mystical voyage into inner space, and although it is admitted that some patients become lost and never emerge, others, especially if they have a guide, come back to our world, their starting point, enriched by new insight. 'Madness need not be all breakdown. It may also be breakthrough. It is potentially liberation and renewal as well as enslavement and existential death.'[122]

Bateson also believes that schizophrenia can be healing for the sufferer, as he writes in his introduction to *Perceval's narrative: a patient's account of his psychosis 1830–1832.*[9]* He argues that, 'This is one of the most interesting characteristics of the strange condition known as schizophrenia: that the disease, if it be one, seems sometimes to have curative properties.'[9]

The illness is regarded as having a course to run, as being like a voyage of discovery by the patient who is seen as the sacrificial victim of a mystifying family.

To evaluate a psychosis is perhaps impossible. Conventionally, schizophrenia is regarded as a disease, and, in terms of this hypothesis, both the conditions necessary for it and the precipitating causes which bring on the attack must be regarded as disastrous. But it would appear that Perceval was a better, happier and more imaginative man after his psychotic experience, and . . . I have suggested that the psychosis is more like some vast and painful initiatory ceremony conducted by the self. From this point of view it is perhaps still reasonable to regard the conditional causes with horror. The precipitating causes can only be welcomed.[9]

Yet despite the brilliance of the psychological understanding of Laing and Bateson, their patients frequently fail to recover. Laing has never claimed better results than those achieved by conventional psychiatry. Perceval was left very strange, despite his allegedly curative illness. This point is difficult to aim against Laing as his

* This Perceval was the son of Spencer Perceval, the only British Prime Minister to have been assassinated, when he was shot in the House of Commons in 1812, by a mentally ill assailant.

stance is cynical about 'cure': he regards cure as itself a sick process, an alienation, part of 'the counter-madness of Kraepelinian psychiatry'. 'Can we not see', he writes, 'that this voyage is not what we need to be cured of, but that it is itself a natural way of healing our own appalling state of alienation called normality?'[123] He also believes that it is a recent phenomenon, perhaps of the last few decades, perhaps of the last 150 years, that society drives people mad, and deprives them of contact with the transcendental and divine. (However, we have seen in Chapter 5 that there have been insane in every age – and in every age there have been worried pessimists proclaiming the shocking increase in madness in their disturbed and sinful times.)

The Laingian point of view is the present-day representative of the age-old tradition of holy madness, the divine inspiration, the prophet and the Delphic oracle. It is a romantic anti-rational view, suspicious of doctors, their knowledge and their efforts, and in its turn uncomprehended by the doctors, from Hippocrates to the psychiatric textbooks of today.

The criticisms of this approach to schizophrenia are scientific, practical and moral.

The scientific criticism is that, as we have seen in Chapter 6, the strongest evidence on the cause of schizophrenia points to heredity and biochemistry, physical matters more likely to be handicapping than of value, and causing breakdown rather than breakthrough. Nevertheless, this does not exclude the possibility that physical processes could induce a state in which the person is receptive to transcendental experiences (are the 'mystical' experiences of LSD 'valid'?). The evidence that schizophrenia is caused by mystifying communication in the family in childhood, or indeed by the impossible demands of modern society, is dubious scientifically at the moment, although the whole body of it impresses me as containing some wisdom unlikely to simply go away.

The practical criticism of these theories of schizophrenia comes from the professional experience of psychiatrists who see and treat the whole gamut of the illness, in interesting and less interesting cases, in brilliant and in mentally handicapped people, in young and old, in developed and developing countries, in our times and in the past. The picture is a grim one of wasted lives, of disability, of unfulfilled potential, of warping of humanity. There is strain, hardship and disappointment imposed on others – parents, children, loved ones, friends. The bright side of the picture is very rare indeed in any kind of person, time or place.

The moral criticism is inevitable in view of this experience: if insanity, in its chief form schizophrenia, is nearly always destructive, and has always been widely regarded as one of the more terrible afflictions of mankind, surely we are not entitled to flirt with a romanticisation of it. I deny that this is a view that is limited and oblivious of the non-rational capabilities of the human spirit, and I cite support from outside the ranks of psychiatrists. The balanced view was held by the literary critic Lionel Trilling, who first establishes concord with the great writers who have seen profundity in madness, but then denies the humanity of glorifying it:

> The impulse to transcend rational mind would seem to be very deeply rooted in man's nature. Before modern anthropology taught us not to despise or condescend to it, the highest literary and philosophical tradition of Western civilization took sympathetic cognizance of it, together with the various means by which it is thought to be realized. Madness, for example, figures memorably in the work of Plato, Shakespeare, Cervantes, Nietzsche, and Yeats, all of whom represent it as a condition productive of truths which are not accessible to our habitual and socially countenanced mode of perception, and constitute an adverse judgement on it. No one is ever in doubt that their representation of madness is of the profoundest and most cogent import, yet no one ever supposes them to be urging upon us that madness, because of the heuristic and moral powers they ascribe to it, is a state of existence which is to be desired and sought for and, as it were, socially established. To say that madness is for them merely a figure of speech would not, I think, state the case accurately. But while their representation of the powers of madness is doubtless something more than a metaphorical construct, it does not ask for credence for the idea that madness is a beneficent condition, to be understood as the paradigm of authentic existence and cognition.

This view is advanced not only by speculative laymen but also by a notable section of post-Freudian psychiatric opinion with wide influence in the intellectual community. The position is argued on grounds which are quite overtly political. The line is taken that insanity is directly related to the malign structures and forces of society, not as a mere passive effect but, rather, as an active and significant response to society's destructive will. Insanity is represented as a true perception appropriately acted out – society itself is insane, and when this is understood, the apparent aberration of the individual appears as rationality, as liberation from the delusions of the social madness. From individual madness, its heartbreaking pain, isolation and distraction blithely ignored, is to be derived the principle by which society may recover its lost reason and humanity. The project may be taken as the measure of how desperate is the impulse to impugn and transcend the limitations of rational mind.[223]

The views on mental illness discussed in this chapter have usually been thought incompatible with the 'medical model' and the research into causes described in the last two chapters. In the next chapter I bring the different theories together and outline a formulation to do justice to all of them.

9
Schizophrenia and madness

Madness is the lay, colloquial term; schizophrenia the professional, psychiatric one. The concept of madness is old; that of schizophrenia is 20th century. The mad have always been with us, as the people who behave outrageously and incomprehensibly, breaking all canons not only of civilised but also of understandable behaviour. To be viewed as madness, this behaviour has to be long-lasting, developing into a style of life, even if an intermittent one, for brief aberrations are seen differently. Violent loss of temper is understood and regarded as such, not as madness. The concepts of temporary loss of control and of madness are normally different, though comparisons are intriguing and lead us to ask how and why madness is different.

Madness is also different from the altered behaviour caused by physical illness disturbing the brain, and lasting for the duration of the illness. Feverish delirium, epilepsy and senility explain peculiar behaviour in terms of ordinary illness, and have done so since the time of Hippocrates. In the present day, all textbooks of psychiatry distinguish between the abnormal behaviour caused by disorder of the brain, and that caused by 'functional psychosis' – that is mental illness, insanity, madness.

Also excluded from madness is behaviour made comprehensible by an obvious motive with which onlookers have a certain amount of sympathy or, at least, intellectual understanding. So, appearing naked in the street, which is outrageous behaviour often taken as *prima facie* evidence of madness, is considered normal if done for a substantial bet, which supplies an acceptable financial incentive, and possibly even if done for publicity (Lady Godiva), or under the influence of fashion and social pressure (the 'streakers' of yesteryear). Drunkenness, causing ordinary disorder of the brain, provides another 'normal' explanation for behaving out of character or beyond the rules that takes priority over the attribution of madness.

Feigning madness for any reason, including the opportunity to hide in a mental hospital or otherwise avoid the responsibility for what one has done, supplies to those in the know an understandable reason for the behaviour in question, and its existence again highlights the importance of the issue of comprehensibility to others in the patient's environment. It is an age-old phenomenon, an early example being the case of King David, who, in terror of King Achish, 'changed his behaviour before them, and feigned himself mad in their hands, and scrabbled on the doors of the gate, and let his spittle fall down upon his beard'.[179]

The term 'schizophrenia' developed in psychiatry from endeavours to subdivide and classify the large number of mentally ill patients in the asylums built by Western countries from the 19th century onwards. There had been earlier schemes of classification of the illnesses in England, Germany and elsewhere, but the first effective and lasting one was that of Kraepelin, who has been regarded ever since as the founder of modern descriptions of the principal illnesses. In his textbook *Psychiatrie*, starting with the fourth edition of 1893, and developing the concept through to the eighth edition of 1909–15, he introduced the description of dementia praecox, recognisably our schizophrenia.

Thus at the beginning of the eighth edition, we read:

Dementia praecox consists of a series of states, the common characteristic of which is a peculiar destruction of the internal connections of the psychic personality. The effects of this injury predominate in the emotional and volitional spheres of mental life . . . Even though in many details there are profound differences of opinion, still the conviction seems to be more and more gaining ground that dementia praecox on the whole represents a well characterised form of disease, and that we are justified in regarding the majority at least of the clinical pictures which are brought together here as the expression of a single morbid process, though outwardly they often diverge very far from one another.[106]

The emphasis in the psychiatric approach is not on incomprehensibility but on mental *illness*, with loss of psychological functions such as the ability to think, feel and act normally.

It appears that this form of mental weakness, in spite of great differences of detail, exhibits many features in common with other forms of dementia, such as are known to us as the results of paralysis, senility or epilepsy. For this reason I have hitherto described under the one name dementia praecox the morbid pictures under consideration. Bleuler [Eugen Bleuler[14]] also has taken them together in his 'group of the schizophrenias' without trying to make a further division of this group.[106]

So, in the first paragraph of Kraepelin's book, the series of states is being called an illness, and at once typical schizophrenic phenomena are described. The patients listen to hallucinatory voices, and there is preoccupation with mysterious action at a distance, as for instance mediated by electricity. The patients talk of being hypnotised and of becoming mediums. One said, 'When I leave the house all the telephones know where I am going and what I am thinking of.'

The schizophrenics described by Kraepelin, Eugen Bleuler[14] and subsequent psychiatry certainly include the typical madmen envisaged by the society of our time. The condition was described in the asylums among the long-term patients, and schizophrenia still dominates the mental hospitals of the world, although in the advanced countries it is slowly yielding place to senile dementia as the most common illness. Despite the improvement in treatment many patients still fare badly, being left severely disabled in personality with more or less grotesque behaviour. Fewer stay in hospital and more are at home, but much handicap remains. The change to an insane way of life, which becomes ingrained, unremitting and does not recover, corresponds to the standard stereotype of mental illness.

As one textbook puts it:

Most of us have encountered conventional descriptions of madness with mythical patients such as the man who believes himself to be a hatstand and remains all day in suitable posture, or the lady who imagines herself to be a teapot and squats with one arm curved like a spout before her and the other hand upon her hip as a handle, constantly asking to be poured out. There are of course no patients as conventionally mad as this, but it is among the chronic deteriorated schizophrenic group that we come most near to seeing pathetic spectacles of this kind. For as their grip upon reality progressively weakens and the content of their minds becomes more primitive, jumbled and chaotic, a few patients may assume and maintain for long periods postures symbolic of some inner stress or experience, just as in the earlier and more acute stages of the illness they may seek to convey to an uncomprehending world otherwise incommunicable feelings and ideas by fantastic gestures, speech and action.[209]

Clearly this qualifies as incomprehensible bizarre behaviour – as madness. However, as well as schizophrenia, there are other conditions described in psychiatry as functional psychoses – major mental illnesses that are not, so far as can be seen at present, caused by ordinary brain disease. Mania and certain severe depressions are classified as psychotic (insane), because the patients change markedly from their former selves, cease to behave reasonably and logically, and may be extreme in their talk and behaviour. Manic patients may be constantly on the move and talking, day and night, until they become hoarse and exhausted. They write reams of letters, flirt coarsely and uninhibitedly, write cheques for millions of pounds and believe that God has granted them boundless powers.

The severely depressed sometimes progress far beyond 'understand-able' misery until they are fixedly convinced that all their money is lost despite evidence to the contrary, and that their bowels are blocked and rotten so that people around them are smelling them and signalling to each other in a code of gestures disguised as ordinary blowing of the nose. Occasionally savage suicides result, based on pessimistic assessments of the situation that are wildly out of tune with the true circumstances. These patients too are mentally ill, but they are not quite so quintessentially 'mad' as the schizophrenics. The manic and the psychotically depressed are not so incomprehensible as the schizophrenics, for the sensitive bystander can feel that the manic patient is living a mere brittle caricature of happiness, and that the severely depressed person has gone to a despair beyond logic and reason as well as (often) beyond tears. We can understand these things, we feel, in a way in which we cannot so simply understand schizophrenics (although Laing has helped considerably with the latter problem, to which *The divided self*[110] is devoted: 'Its basic purpose is to make madness, and the process of going mad, compre-hensible . . . I wanted to convey above all that it was far more possible than is generally supposed to understand people diagnosed as psychotic').

Manfred Bleuler, one of the most distinguished and experienced of living students of schizophrenia (and the son of Eugen Bleuler), summarises the results of his lifetime's devotion to research on the subject as follows:

(1) The patients are not physically ill.
(2) The state is experienced subjectively as a problem between the patient's own being and his experience of life.
(3) This agrees with our own observations of their difficulties.
(4) There are no environmental stresses in the past lives of schizo-phrenics which are specific ones for the development of this condition.
(5) There are hereditary factors, but we do not understand how they work.
(6) The (frequently pre-existing) schizoid personality itself

represents a lack of harmony between the person and the events of his life.

(7) Schizophrenic ways of experiencing and thinking occur in a hidden form in the mentally healthy, and similarly healthy ways of experiencing and thinking remain in a hidden way preserved in schizophrenia.

(8) The schizophrenic patient does not dement [i.e. undergo depletion of mental functions through deterioration of the cerebral processes] – a rich inner life remains.

(9) After some five years on the average there is no further deterioration, and more often some improvement takes place.

(10) All the methods of treatment help by reaching the healthy parts of the personality.

In addition, 'The schizophrenic loses himself in the discord between the disharmony of his own personality and the disharmony of his environment.'[15] Bleuler's formulation goes on to suggest that an inherited disposition, perhaps to a disharmony of development, leads to a complementary disharmony in human relationships. Then, at some point, new stresses cause a break in which adaptation to the world of other people becomes impossible. He summarises: 'In my opinion the schizophrenic happening takes place in the realms of the mind and the emotions, that is, in mental spheres that exist only in man.'[15]

This agrees with the findings of the research on causes, discussed in Chapter 6, in which no definite physical cause has been found, although the established hereditary predisposition must, of course, be handed on by a physical mechanism, through the genes. Even psychiatrists who feel sure that schizophrenia is an illness with physical causes admit that it is a different *type* of illness from the undisputed cerebral dysfunctions of epilepsy, high fever, cerebral anoxia, senile dementia, and others. This is the reason for the separate categories for organic (i.e. cerebrally based) illnesses and functional psychoses, the severe mental illnesses, especially schizophrenia.

There is agreement about the use of 'psychosis' as a description, and even those who see schizophrenia as an understandable defensive strategy do not classify it as a neurosis, or as a more direct reaction to the stress of life. M. Bleuler says, 'There is no schizophrenia without psychosis,' and in his list of 14 generally agreed points in diagnosing schizophrenia, the first one states that it is a psychosis or mental illness.[16] Lidz writes: 'The critical attribute of the category of psychoses termed "schizophrenia" lies in the aberrant symbolic processes – the distortions of perception, meaning and logic – that occur without degradation of intellectual potential.'[136]

Lidz construes the condition as a desperate withdrawal (see Ch. 7):

> Schizophrenic reactions are a type of withdrawal from social inter-
> action, and the thought disorder is a specifically schizophrenic
> means of withdrawal . . . The schizophrenic patient escapes from
> irreconcilable dilemmas and unbearable hopelessness by breaking
> through these confines [i.e. the meanings and logic of his culture] to
> find some living space by using his own idiosyncratic meanings and
> reasoning, but in so doing impairs his ego-functioning and ability to
> collaborate with others.[136]

Laing, whose understanding of many of these patients has been
more profound than that of anyone else, nevertheless had repeatedly
to call them psychotic in *The divided self.*[114]

Physical changes may be found in the future as markers or even as
the underlying cause of schizophrenia, but this is not the case at the
moment. All the diagnostic criteria are descriptions of behaviour or
the patients' reports of their own experiences, and none is a disturbance of the physiology of the body. This in turn means that the
criteria of abnormality are social, concerning the degree of aberrant
behaviour regarded as abnormal in society, as interpreted by society's
appointed watchdogs of the boundaries of madness, the psychiatrists.

Schizophrenia is thus seen by those doctors who try to construe it
with some meaning, and who do not regard it as a biochemical
disorder, as a dislocation between the inner world of the person and
the outer world. It is a serious mental illness, with disruption of the
usual processes of perception, thinking, feeling and action. It is a
madness, because the patients behave incomprehensibly in the eyes of
the rest of society. It has a beginning, a course, sometimes an end
with healing, and sometimes a permanent disability compared with
the original personality.

It is in fact an *illness* that disables the sufferer by dislocating the
relationship between his inner self and the outside world.

Some physical causes for syndromes resembling schizophrenia have
been found as described in Chapter 6, for example, abuse of
amphetamines in large doses, and some cases of temporal lobe
epilepsy, but these are then not regarded as true schizophrenia. The
concept of schizophrenia refers to the remaining cases, idiopathic in
medical terminology, that is of unknown cause. They correspond
approximately to the 'residual' deviance of Scheff,[183] after other
known causes of deviance have been allowed for.

Schizophrenia is thus an area within the concept of madness. The
terms have different disciplinary origins – madness as incomprehensible deviance from social rules; schizophrenia as a disabling syndrome

of particular behaviour, described by doctors – but, in fact, all schizophrenics are mad and none are sane.

The sociological and psychiatric viewpoints can be compared as follows:

Society defines	**madness**	seen as	**incomprehensible deviant behaviour**	requiring	**segregation and control or correction**
| decides the doctors' role, and |					
Doctors define	**schizo-phrenia**	seen as	**mental illness**	requiring	**medical treatment for cure** (albeit sometimes involuntary, segregated and controlling)

Four theories

Four theories of schizophrenia and madness are current: the neurological, the psychiatric, the sociological and the prophetic. They are different from each other, but overlap.

According to the *neurological* view, schizophrenia is a disorder of the brain, a disease. This is the point of view of many psychiatrists, including most in the 19th century and many at the present time. For example, the principal textbook of psychiatry in Britain for the last 30 years, by Slater and Roth, after stating that schizophrenia comprises a group of mental illnesses characterised by specific psychological symptoms, continues: 'If these primary symptoms are present, then they are features which refute any purely psychogenic theory.'[204] Theories have included those of a biochemical and hereditary basis (for which, as we have seen, there is good evidence), and other surprising suggestions espoused energetically in the absence of evidence, such as the current theories for an involvement of food allergy, immune disorders, virus disease or cell senility.

In these theories, the disorder is of course a medical one, and doctors will be required to understand and treat it. What the patients say and do is viewed as the essentially distorted and jumbled communications of a disordered brain. The behaviour is incomprehensible, or at least gives no fresh insight into the human condition.

The syndrome is seen as a kind of unusually productive delirium, and interesting things that the patients say as accidental epiphenomena, no more profound than dysphasic speech after a stroke, or the productions of the early states of dementia in syphilitic general paralysis. This theory is entrenched in psychiatric philosophy, the commonest conception of schizophrenia being that it is a 'functional psychosis', a serious disorder not (yet) attributable to brain disease, but expected to be so attributable one day (often thought to be soon).

According to the *psychiatric* theory, schizophrenia is a mental disorder, a malfunction of the life of the mind, and thus potentially of psychological interest, although it loses comprehensibility because it is a breakdown, a disorganisation. In this view it is *neither* brain disease *nor* straightforward reaction to stress like mild depression or neurosis, but in a rather mysterious category of its own. It is an illness, but a mental one. This is the metaphorical illness on the analogy of physical disease, so often criticised, especially by Szasz in *The myth of mental illness*.[212]

Murphy's theory that schizophrenia is visionary thinking gone out of control is psychiatric.[154] So also are the theories of M. Bleuler, quoted above, of Ciompi[26] ('it more closely resembles a life process . . . than an illness with a given course'), and of Lidz who regards it as a desperate and handicapping withdrawal 'in the nature of illusion and delusion, [with] very little to do with anything real or practical . . . [it] tends to be a self-perpetuating condition in which people give up validating their experience'.[135]

The psychiatric viewpoint is partly shared by Laing in *The divided self*,[115] where he mentions psychosis and crossing the border into insanity (although he also espouses its social definition[113] and discusses labelling).

According to the *sociological* theory, madness is a social role, a form of deviance, probably with functions in society and certainly only to be understood in social terms (and fully comprehensible in these terms). The psychiatric profession is considered to be participating in a process of 'medicalising' deviance by saying it is a form of illness, a (mythical) mental illness. It may be conceded that some of the disordered behaviour may be initially determined by illness or at least by severe mental or behavioural dysfunction, but this is thought to be less important than the response of society to the deviancy.

Versions of this theory have been espoused by Becker ('Social groups create deviance by making rules whose infraction constitutes deviance');[11] Lemert, in his analysis of labelling;[133,134] Scheff;[183] Szasz[212,214] (see Ch. 8 of this book); and by Laing at times when he discusses labelling;[120,121] and, in fact, it is the orthodox view of sociology.

Bastide says that, 'The isolation which for some psychiatrists characterises the world of the mentally ill is merely the translation, in morphological terms, of the marginality of values that have been rejected or repressed by the rest of society . . . Clearly one is insane only in relation to a particular society.'⁷

A fourth theory sees madness as at least sometimes *akin to prophecy*, offering comments and sometimes the most profound insight into society and the human condition. This is an offshoot of the sociological theory, for it ignores the possibility of illness, and regards prophecy as a social institution. Madness is only incomprehensible to the benighted or unimaginative, because it is too deep for them. Psychiatrists, moreover, are usually among the insensitive who miss the message.

The tradition of divine madness is ancient and widespread. In Chapter 5, I cited its description by Plato and mentioned examples of it in other times. In our time, adherents to the tradition see the madmen as alienated from their families and society as a whole. This is the viewpoint of Laing, especially in *The politics of experience* with its introduction on alienation[118] and mention of healing possibilities in psychosis,[122] and of Bateson in the introduction to *Perceval's narrative*.[9] It is the view criticised in my quotation from Trilling,[223] who recognises flashes of profundity but denies any reason for glorification of insanity. The sociological and prophetic viewpoints have also been those of many anthropologists studying exotic cultures, including Murphy (see Ch. 4) before her field work changed her mind. Bastide gives a sociological yet partially prophetic view, in saying that the isolation

> represents an effort to find a 'niche' in the structure of social space, where [marginal] values can hide and vegetate, and where they can defend themselves by secreting a shell which finally reduces to its bare existential minimum what it was intended to preserve . . . The madman is to a certain extent the expression of our guilty conscience; he represents the chaotic part of ourselves that we wish to negate, exteriorized and operating in public . . . Madness . . . enables us to free ourselves by transferring to others the dangers that threaten us. The madman may bear within him the human condition, but normal man is the seed-bed in which madness takes root.⁸

I believe that the evidence and arguments supporting the different viewpoints are not so incompatible as has often been maintained. Although the areas of ignorance are very great, we can go some way towards the 'New Synthesis' mentioned as his goal by Wing in the title of his book but not found inside its covers.[235] I shall sketch the outline of a formulation of schizophrenia in the next section.

A formulation

It is generally agreed that we are very far from understanding schizo-phrenia, and the accumulation of knowledge proceeds very slowly. I have indicated that the strongest scientific evidence points to a hereditary contribution to the cause, and to familial and drug influences on the liability to relapse. The familial theories of cause are, in the main, strictly speculative.

We are also ignorant of the extent to which schizophrenia may be a group of conditions, misleading to discuss together because different patients may be suffering from separate illnesses with separate causes. Perhaps the totally unsatisfactory results of our efforts to subdivide the whole field can account for the conflicting views on its cause.

Nevertheless, despite the fragmentary state of our knowledge I wish to attempt a formulation and put together as many pieces as possible of the jigsaw puzzle to suggest the outline of a picture.

The parents

The established evidence for true genetic transmission of schizo-phrenia described in Chapter 6 shows that the parents often, and quite possibly always, pass on to the children genes that carry a vulner-ability to schizophrenia and also the schizoid state of personality, which may include creative forms of eccentricity. Fathers and mothers have equal effect in the heredity of schizophrenia.

The parents are also likely to be the principal environmental influ-ences in the familial clustering of schizophrenia. The theories, per-suasive but short on scientific evidence, were discussed in Chapter 7. Experience of the patients and their families, and consideration of the theories of sensitive and profound psychiatrists, convince me that the styles of communication in the family when the schizophrenics were young must have something to do with the transmission of irrationality and schizophrenia, even though no specificity has been found for these styles in comparison with those in other unhappy families. It is certain that the parents are, more frequently than would be expected, unusual (often schizoid) in personality, unhappily married, and, of course, liable themselves to suffer from schizophrenia (and therefore from highly odd modes of communication). Probably there is a dimension of clouded communication in the family, irrational and even mystifying, a phenomenon which so many have tried to describe from different viewpoints and in different terms.

As we shall see, the future patients are often detectably abnormal as children, so it is important to note that no evidence has yet disproved the possibility that most of the abnormalities of communication come *after*, and in response to, the experience of bringing up an abnormal child.

The pre-schizophrenic child

As children, future schizophrenics show many signs of handicap in both physical and psychological capacities. Comparisons with control children and with non-schizophrenic co-twins in twin births show that the pre-schizophrenics had more obstetric problems at birth, lower birth weight and poorer health in childhood.

Psychologically, the theories of family mystification, intrusion and cold over-protectiveness maintain that, in enduring the 'double-bind' and other mechanisms, the child is forced to develop alienated attitudes and irrational styles to protect himself.

Watt made a study of the school records of schizophrenics, written years before any mental illness was suspected, and found many abnormalities in the teachers' descriptions.

The boys were more negativistic, less conscientious and less stable than control boys. They were, in fact, actively maladjusted, while the girls were quietly maladjusted, passive and immature, and less stable than control girls. The children in Watt's study had no academic deficiencies, but also no friends.

If a single expression can capture the essence of a pattern of results so complex as this one, it is *emotional immaturity* . . . There were frequent references to 'crying with slight provocation', being overshadowed by older siblings, insensitivity to the feelings of others, late development of physical and scholastic skills, temper outbursts, and self-consciousness. The introversion of the girls and the extreme alienation of the boys, especially in later childhood, seem like natural outgrowths of a history of retarded emotional development.'[228]

The experience of being the parent of such a child is sure to be stressful, even mystifying, and may contribute to the unhappiness and over-protectiveness already noted in the parents. A vicious circle may be set up, with a physically and emotionally immature child of schizoid, unhappy parents calling forth natural protective responses which are seen by researchers, and may be felt by the child, as cold intrusion, causing withdrawal, alienation, more strangeness, more labelling as strange, and further protectiveness.

Schizoid personality and pre-schizophrenia

Rarely does schizophrenia come out of the blue: usually some schizoid traits of personality have been noted, and even in the cases with acute explosive onset there has nearly always been a secret inner eccentricity behind a facade of relative normality presented to the outside world (Laing gives examples of this[115]). The schizoid personality is a description of a person in a degree of alienation short of psychosis. Stafford-Clark and Smith gave the following psychiatric definition: 'While it is certainly true that cold, potentially ruthless dreamy eccentrics, or lonely diffident sensitive and suspicious people, may often be described as displaying schizoid traits, it is their inability to deal successfully with external reality, and especially intimacy with other people, which links them in practice.'[209]

Wolff and Chick defined the condition using these characteristics:[239]

solitariness (few close relationships – this affects sexual life and makes marriage uncommon)

impaired sympathy and emotional detachment

increased sensitivity (in the sense of touchiness, being thin-skinned)

rigidity of mental set (fixed views, rarely change opinion, sometimes single-mindedly pursue a specific interest)

unusual or odd style of communication (woolly, circumstantial, tangential, uncommunicative or over-talkative).

The finest descriptions are those of Laing in *The divided self,*[110] and of Dostoyevsky when he describes Raskolnikov in *Crime and punishment,*[43] with other examples in *The outsider.*[232]

The solitariness, which leaves some schizoid people unmarried, reminds us that schizophrenics marry considerably less often than healthy people of their age, and so have fewer children. If schizophrenia were indeed a partly hereditary illness, the genes for schizophrenic vulnerability in the population would die out as generations of childless individuals succeeded each other, unless other factors increasing the gene population were acting at the same time. One possibility could be that the gene pool is increased in each generation by mutation at a rate which balances the loss of genes caused by the lack of children. It is not known if this is so. A more likely explanation is a *balanced polymorphism* by which the severe biological disadvantage to the species of the childless schizophrenics is balanced by the slight biological advantage of the more common schizoid personalities. What could be the breeding advantage to the species of minor degrees of schizophrenic heredity, manifest as slightly schizoid personality? One possibility is that the degree of detachment could encourage originality of thinking, and creativity. A modest quantum of schizo-phrenic heredity might result in all the advantages of originality without the emotional detachment from people which lowers the likelihood of marrying and having children. The original and creative people would be successful in survival to adult life and in sexual selection, and could be at least as fertile as the general population, thus ensuring the perpetuation of their genes. This remains a hypothesis with no supporting evidence for advantageous fertility, but the suggestion that the schizoid personality can be associated with creativity is supported by evidence such as that of Heston mentioned in Chapter 6,[74] and by experience. So, Storr[210] suggests that creative activity is a particularly apt way for the schizoid individual to express himself, and explains why (see Ch. 7).

An illuminating story of father and child, schizoid and schizo-phrenic, is that of James Joyce and his daughter, Lucia. In his biography of Joyce, Richard Ellman says of Jung's treatment of Lucia for severe schizophrenia: 'When the psychologist pointed out schizoid elements in poems Lucia had written, Joyce, remembering Jung's comment on *Ulysses,* insisted they were anticipations of a new literature, and said his daughter was an innovator not yet understood. Jung granted that some of her portmanteau words and neologisms were remarkable, but said they were random; she and her father, he commented later, were like two people going to the bottom of a river, one falling and the other diving.'[48]

Jung's own words on Joyce were: 'His "psychological" style is definitely schizophrenic, with the difference, however, that the ordinary patient cannot help talking and thinking in such a way, while Joyce willed it and moreover developed it with all his creative forces.'[100]

Becoming psychotic

Crider says of pre-schizophrenic children: 'They tend to see them-selves as driven by uncontrollable impulses and urges, as friendless in a rejecting and hostile world, as increasingly retarded *vis-à-vis* peers in social–emotional development. Low self-esteem begins to merge with the harbingers of psychotic breakdown: hallucinatory experience, depersonalization, delusions of control by others, and experiences of derealization.'[39]

When a person becomes psychotic, either new processes must be involved, or older ones must gather fresh momentum and become for a time irreversible. In a few cases, physical factors affecting the brain are known to be acting: prolonged intake of large doses of amphetamine, and occasionally alcohol, hallucinogenic drugs, or long-continued epilepsy especially in the temporal lobe of the brain. There is recent research suggesting that, with the latest techniques, slight cerebral changes can be detected in more schizophrenics than was thought, a promising finding for the expanding field of brain research.[103] Usually no physical disorders are detected, but they may well be operating nevertheless: the fact that heredity must act through molecular chemistry, discoveries in the field of neurotransmitters in the brain in health and disease, and the extraordinary fact that only a few millionths of a gram of LSD can profoundly alter the state of mind and bring about hallucinations suggest that biochemical discoveries relevant to the causes of schizophrenia are extremely likely to be made in the future, even if it seems unlikely, as it does to me, that they will tell the whole story.

Psychological and social factors impinging on the individual during his slide into schizophrenia include those discussed in Chapter 7. The influences which may operate in childhood, especially the emotional attitude of the parents, continue into adult life. If there is criticism and rejection of a patient who remains in his family, he may feel over-bombarded with social communication, while his protective perceptual filters are faulty. He is in the double-bind of Bateson's theory, which appears as the carefully scored critical remarks of the patient's relatives in the research at the Institute of Psychiatry, London.[10,128]

Additional stress occurs in the weeks before overt psychosis, and schizophrenics are extremely sensitive to outside stimulation despite outward appearances sometimes to the contrary. Adverse life events (and even putatively happy events, perhaps over-stimulating) can be counted and found in excess before the breakdown, but the innumerable vagaries of life also continue, uncounted. The young schizophrenics are, with their immature resources, facing adolescence while still with their families. The older face other personal demands on them; in the elderly the sensory deprivation of social isolation and deafness increase the withdrawal into disordered inner life.

The withdrawal becomes more severe, and the mental abnormalities begin. Thinking becomes over-private and idiosyncratic in words, syntax, symbols and style, and uncoupled from logical trains of thought. This is schizophrenic thought-disorder, described in Chapter 3. Beliefs become over-private, desperately defensive and independent of the facts of the outside world: delusions. Perceptions become over-private, so that thoughts may be indistinguishable from them: hallucinations. (The fact that hallucinations are most often of hearing voices, and less often of visions, smells or touches, emphasises the importance of disorders of spoken communication, and of the attitude to them in schizophrenia.) Emotion becomes over-private, too: there are secret unexpected laughter and tears, termed 'emotional incongruity' by psychiatry; or it may be largely inconspicuous to others, the so-called 'flattening of affect'.

The illness seems to be not an ordered withdrawal but a disordered flight from the outer world, involving a pathological and disabling process of disruption at the boundary between inner and outer worlds. The typical symptoms of the feeling of thoughts being inserted into the mind from outside, of thoughts being broadcast to the world with terrifying loss of privacy, and of the body and personality being controlled and manipulated by strange forces (witchcraft, electricity, radiation, hypnosis, telepathy) illustrate this loss of awareness of a boundary between on the one hand, the patient, and what he thinks and controls, and on the other, the rest of the world.

The reaction of society

The evidence discussed before gives reasons for much of the development of schizophrenia in individuals, and I do not think that the condition is best accounted for by the extreme sociological theory of labelling, which maintains that very slight and unimportant deviations from the norm – oddities of behaviour in this case – become magnified by the labelling process when attention is drawn to them, and that the insane role is then adopted by some of those caught up in the labelling process. Even if the social explanation is found illuminating, psychological explanations in the individual, or explanations relating to his unique environment, are needed to account for the vulnerability and selection of the individual who comes to represent the social process. (This is the usual problem of the interaction of social and psychological explanations for individual behaviour: e.g. changes in morals and methods of display in shops increase the frequency of shoplifting, but personal reasons can be sought for any individual's committing the offence.)

The responses of family, workmates and society at large to the oddity and rule-breaking of the schizophrenic, even if they are not causative of the original behaviour, certainly have major effects on the course of the illness. One possible response of society is the institution of prophecy that accepts a wide range of unusual behaviour and may honour and revere individuals reporting unusual experiences of altered states of consciousness. The Hebrew prophets of the Old Testament are the best examples, especially Ezekiel, described in Chapter 5. It is often maintained that this also happens in many traditional tribal cultures through such institutions as shamanism, voodoo and witch-doctors, although I have quoted Murphy in Chapter 4 in support of my view that this is not usually the case on closer examination. The shamans are found to be pursuing a profession and have little in common with the handicapping withdrawal and inability to think and perceive clearly of the schizophrenic. The argument that it is the absence of a role for the holy madman in our society that has driven the patient into the deteriorated rejected state is invalid, because of the evidence that typical cases of schizophrenia are found, in about the same frequency, virtually all over the world, in very disparate cultures.[36,220]

The second group of reactions of the social environment to the schizophrenic occur when he is regarded as abnormal, being at least eccentric or else insane, but able to remain in the community. The labelling in the family or neighbourhood leads to the stigma of mental illness being applied in ever wider circumstances. Straightforward actions may be quoted as confirmatory evidence of mental illness by fearful bystanders. Temper becomes 'abnormal violence'; hints, humour and obliquity of utterance become incomprehensibility; going for a walk becomes 'wandering away'; deep thinking becomes 'withdrawal'. The expectations become self-fulfilling: they drive the patient into further alienation, which provides more evidence of oddity, which confirms the family view that there is something wrong with his mind . . .

> There must be something the matter with him
> because he would not be acting as he does
> unless there was
> therefore he is acting as he is
> because there is something the matter with him
> He does not think there is anything the matter with him because
> one of the things that is
> the matter with him
> is that he does not think there is anything
> the matter with him
> Therefore
> we have to help him realize that
> the fact that he does not think there is anything
> the matter with him
> is one of the things that is
> the matter with him.[124]

The schizophrenic enters the social role of madness in his culture, known in ordinary folk-lore from childhood onwards, and his schizophrenia, the basic phenomena of which are universal in all cultures, becomes flavoured by madness as he and his family know, or think they know, it happens. In Western cultures, it is mad to talk to yourself, as every schoolboy knows, or to run in the street naked, so some patients do this, and so does an occasional malingerer pretending to be insane.

Playing the mad role increases the social handicaps of the original schizophrenic process, and the typical downward drift in society begins. Wing describes it as:

> a pattern in which early timidity and shyness, loss of peer relation-ships in adolescence, poor school performance and early work record, reduction in social status and, finally, migration into a decaying, disorganized urban area, tend to occur as successive stages in the life-histories of pre-schizophrenic individuals.[236]

According to Scott,[189] at this point in the family life of the patient, a sudden 'closure' occurs, designating him as insane in the eyes of the rest of the family for ever more, whether or not he himself agrees with this designation. The parent (who may recall irrationality in his own parents) cannot go on sharing family life if his child claims to be normal and suggests that the parent is the abnormal one. This becomes an 'untenable' situation for the parent, and he insists that the child be admitted to hospital, where he usually remains for a long time. If the parent is acknowledged by the child to be well, and particularly if the child capitulates to the diagnosis of being ill himself, the group may continue to live together in the community.

The third social result is admission to an institution of the psychiatric service – formerly a lunatic asylum, now a mental hospital or less commonly (one-third of psychiatric admissions, and probably a lower proportion of schizophrenics, in Great Britain in the early 1980s) a psychiatric ward in a general hospital. There is public knowledge of his having been sent away to join the insane, and the effects of the institution and its stigma begin (recounted in Rosenhan's experiment,[177] described in Chapter 8, and especially in Goffman's *Asylums*,[63] due allowance being required for its being set over 20 years ago in a state hospital in the United States). The deprived social environment and all-pervading expectations of insanity in poor neglected psychiatric wards increase the social disabilities of the schizophrenic patient. Further vicious circles are set up: those who are visited by relatives in the early weeks are more likely to be dis-charged before long, whereas those who are in less contact with the outside world lose their points of reference, become more disabled and are less likely to leave. These matters are described more fully in *Institutional neurosis* by Russell Barton,[6] and in *Institutionalism and schizophrenia* by Wing and Brown.[237]

Long-stay patients suffer the most severe deterioration, although the worst states that were common in mental hospitals until 20–30 years ago – long-term tube feeding, total withdrawal into statuesque silence, or muttering, huddled figures in shapeless, filthy clothes on the floor of long gloomy corridors – are now rare.

In this theory, the illness may be the pathological end of a process which starts as one variety of human adaptive possibility. The genetic vulnerability must have some evolutionary advantage when it is mild in degree, presumably in the capacity of thoughtful, detached individuals to be judicious, original and successful. Cerebral, familial and social processes contribute pressure to retreat from the outer world to the inner, from public to private, and from reason to unreason. All combinations of the risk factors are found in different individual cases of schizophrenia, including, in our present state of knowledge, no identifiable ones at all in some cases, whose genesis remains a complete mystery.

In the individual patient, the early stages are followed by loss of control of mental functioning, usually with total loss of creativity, and often leading to severe disablement. The victims are lost, not waving but drowning.

10

Treatment today

In 'Other times' and 'Other places', I described schizophrenia and madness in settings very different from our own, and touched on some different efforts to help the victims. In general, attitudes have ranged between, on the one hand, rejection of the patient from society as horrifying and intolerable and, on the other, recognition of the need for arrangements for decent care of an awkward but often tragically disabled fellow man. These different ways of thinking have continued into our own time, when the patient, his family, the neighbours, the policeman, the judge, the philanthropist, the sociologist, the nurse and the doctor all have different suggestions and moral approaches. I give a short account of one approach and its ramifications: the provision of good psychiatric services and treatment.

In the community or in hospital?

Asylums and hospitals have always been prominent in the arrangements for the care of schizophrenics, ensuring that the patients are, at the very least, out of harm's way and able to be controlled and at best, cared for or cured by attendants or the nursing, medical and related professions. Outside hospital, schizophrenics can be severely neglected, often homeless, found wandering, verminous or even frozen to death in cold weather. Even in family homes or bedsitting rooms they can become filthy and emaciated while tormented by their illness.

Yet the disadvantages of admission to hospital have been much emphasised. The large and neglected asylums of former years offered an impoverished life in grossly abnormal surroundings that probably increased the intrinsic handicaps of the illness and certainly had little curative effect.

The process of diagnosing the patient as mentally ill and recommending his admission is the major step in the social processes discussed in Chapter 8. He is already the abnormal member of the family in the eyes of relatives, and then is labelled as deviant and mentally ill in the eyes of society when he behaves oddly in public. His strange behaviour is then described to the psychiatrist, and an irreversible process is set in motion: ever after the admission he will be the ex-mental hospital patient in the eyes of his family, doctors, employers, life insurance companies, immigration officials and anyone else who discovers what has happened to him. However, if the whole family is regarded as disturbed, and not merely the patient, then his admission to hospital is to be avoided, as it prevents future dealings with the whole family as equals from succeeding, for not all members will be on an equal footing. After his admission the patient will be in an inferior position, a marked man.

Yet even when the family and society are pressing surprisingly strongly for his admission to hospital, it may be in his interests to recommend rather than resist it. Admission will remove him from the stressful environment and allow a period for reconsideration and settling down, a 'moratorium'[139] on what has been happening to him. In this limited sense of leaving his environment for a more suitable one, many different places of shelter would suffice, and the patient need not necessarily go to a hospital. This is one reason why hostels and communities have been set up by the social services authorities and charitable organisations.

In practice, most schizophrenics are admitted to hospital in their first illness, usually without legal arrangements and merely on the psychiatrist's advice. Success with outpatient or day patient care throughout the illness is uncommon. However, most of the patients admitted greatly improve in a few weeks or months, and then plans for return to the community need to be considered.

Compulsory admission of unwilling patients*

All civilised countries need legislation providing for and governing the compulsory admission to hospital of those seriously insane who refuse to go voluntarily. Resort to compulsory action is quite rare and most patients can be persuaded to be treated in hospital without legal formalities, if the psychiatric service is readily accessible in local general hospitals (where one-third of psychiatric admissions now take place); if the professional staff tend to be known to the patient and his family, as is usually the case with the British family practitioner; and if the law is so framed as to encourage simple forms of admission, as does the British Mental Health Act of 1959. In England, 90 per cent of psychiatric patients are now admitted completely without

---

* Some changes in the law are expected with the passage of the Mental Health (Amendment) Act, 1982.

formalities, only 10 per cent being legally compelled. This figure for voluntary admission is already creditably high when compared with that in other countries, and is still rising. However, vigilance is required lest in future the psychiatrists retreat before the increasing legal formalities being demanded by the lobby for civil liberties, and allow patients to stay in the community free, but neglected. In Britain there are orders lasting for 72 hours or 28 days,* and rare long-lasting orders admitting patients for treatment for up to a year. The long orders for mental illness are, in adults over the age of 21, largely applied to schizophrenia.

The patients may be utterly alienated from, or out of touch with, everyday conventions. They may break all rules of behaviour, turn night into day, neglect themselves dangerously (as did Mr A. R; see Ch. 2), ignore table manners and decent dress, masturbate in public or act dangerously on delusions of persecution (as did Daniel McNaughton; see Ch. 5). They may proclaim their distress, yet be inaccessible to advice about treatment. They may even break the rules about how to break rules: they may draw no income because they will not have themselves regarded as sick, nor sign on as unemployed, yet may live off elderly parents; they may give neighbours an impossible life without contravening the criminal law. Relatives despair at their inability to insist on getting help.

When the reason for the compulsory admission is the patient's own welfare, the concern is over possible suicide or self-mutilation, dangerous neglect, or decline into increasingly severe disability. When it is the family or neighbours who need to be protected, however, compulsory admission is regarded by extreme libertarians like Szasz[214] as a form of police action to suppress or remove an awkward person, and disgraceful if masquerading as an action based on concern for the patient's health. The move is nevertheless prompted by medical humane considerations: to get treatment for a treatable illness. The psychiatrist, in deciding to recommend admission, is encouraged by the prospect of cure in hospital for acute cases who would at home refuse treatment and remain inaccessible. He is discouraged in more chronic cases if treatment in hospital is known to have failed before, and the patient has mainly long-lasting disabilities.

The legal criteria under the Mental Health Act[208] for the 72-hour emergency orders (Section 29 of the Act) and the 28-day observation orders (Section 25) are that the patient shall be suffering from 'mental disorder, of a nature or degree which warrants [i.e. is sufficiently severe to justify] the detention of the patient in a hospital under

---

* In England and Wales. In Scotland there is only one form of short order, for 7 days.

observation (with or without other medical treatment) for at least a limited period; and that he ought to be so detained in the interests of his own health or safety or with a view to the protection of other persons'. In the treatment orders (Section 26), lasting up to a year, the wording of the last section is stronger: detention for treatment 'is necessary in the interests of the patient's health or safety, or for the protection of other persons'. Thus, the reasons are common-sense criteria justifying intervention, and the law expressly forbids over-zealous arrangements for admission, by stating that to suffer from mental illness is on its own insufficient ground for compulsory admission: the condition must also be severe and of a type to justify further the grave step of removing the civil liberties of the patient.

The agents who may make arrangements for compulsory admission are, in England and Wales, except in the 72-hour orders, two doctors, one of whom must be a psychiatrist; in addition confirmation that it is desirable to act on the doctors' recommendations must be supplied by one non-medical person acting in the patient's interests. This person can be the nearest relative or can be a social worker if no relative is available or ready to act. He interviews the patient after the doctors have examined him, and decides whether to apply to a hospital authority to take him in. In the emergency 72-hour orders, the minimum procedure is examination by any one doctor and application for admission by any relative or social worker. Although the patient loses his freedom, the courts are not involved if there is no criminal charge, and this is an indication of the extent to which the law of the United Kingdom confirms the medical context as the correct one for insanity.

Psychotherapy

Individual dynamic psychotherapy has never been regarded as the treatment of choice for schizophrenia; psychoanalysts and others in their tradition usually find the patients too disturbed to be able to enter treatment fruitfully. They are thought to have difficulty in forming a relationship with the analyst, so that the crucial analysis of the unconscious sources of this relationship cannot take place. There have been exceptions to this rule, including famous cases of analysis of schizophrenic patients, for example those of Sechehaye.[195] Arieti has continued to advocate psychotherapy as the main form of treatment,[2] and it has gained support from Laing's writings,[110,126] but usually the enterprise has been regarded as not only too difficult, but also as hazardous – for patient and therapist. Therapists can lose their way in the uncharted depths of the psychotic mind, and patients can easily be made worse by being encouraged to immerse themselves more deeply in their already preoccupying and disturbing fantasies. Lidz[136] says that attempts at psychotherapy should not use the free association of classical psychoanalysis, but whichever interventions can reduce the patient's overwhelming anxiety (and he says that drugs may help at the same time because they simultaneously reduce anxiety). The influential Sullivan[211] in America has given similar advice about the need for an open, supportive, approach, in which the therapist avoids obscure comments and remains as simple, approachable and confidence-inspiring as possible.

Results are hard to assess, because psychotherapists report small numbers of patients, select those (favourable) cases whom they wish to treat, and, especially in America, have used a broad definition of the illness regarded in most other countries as including less ill and even non-psychotic people.

Psychiatrists who think that family relationships cause schizophrenic disorders have advocated forms of family therapy intended to expose and modify the double-binds, mystification and scapegoating of the patient that they find. They use their familiarity with the usual themes and undercurrents in these families to interpret the coded messages by what is sometimes guesswork, but may be successful, although it may on occasion temporarily increase distress. Family themes continue when the patient is in hospital: for example, anxious and disturbing visits from a mother may, in the course of revealing discussions, turn out to be an expression of her uncertainty about whether she can bear to survive without the patient who has been removed from home.

There are three main reasons why psychotherapy has not been a principal form of treatment. One is the widespread conviction that schizophrenia is a serious illness, a process, possibly caused by a disorder of the brain, and therefore *a priori* unlikely to be influenced by a mere talking therapy. The second is the experience of many psychotherapists that it is simply too difficult to help schizophrenics. The third is the evidence of scientific research on comparisons of different methods of treatment; in these it has been shown repeatedly that formal psychotherapy contributes very little to the improvement of the condition in comparison with drug treatment. This research will be described below.

These remarks apply only when interpretive psychotherapy in the psychoanalytic tradition is the main treatment; they do not imply that understanding and sometimes profound relationships with doctors, psychiatric nurses and other professional and lay people are not important in the care of the patients: on the contrary, they are indispensable.

Drugs

Sedatives and hypnotic drugs such as barbiturates have not been found helpful in treatment. Tranquillizers that relieve anxiety, such as the benzodiazepine drugs (diazepam (proprietary name, Valium), chlordiazepoxide (Librium), and their relatives), somewhat surprisingly, in view of the aroused and frightened state of many of the patients, bring little relief and certainly no lasting benefit. Propranolol (Inderal), principally used in damping down the activity of the autonomic nervous system to relieve heart disease, has been tried in schizophrenia: a few early results were promising, but there are signs that it will not establish itself as a useful form of treatment. Treatment with insulin is obsolete. Enthusiastic claims for cures with huge doses of vitamins or by altering the patients' diet have never been confirmed when tested by other doctors.

It is drugs of quite different types that have greatly improved the acute treatment and prevention of relapse in recent years.[57] There are many of them in use, a list of the principal ones being as follows:

	Usual dosage
phenothiazines:	
chlorpromazine (Largactil)	100–800 mg daily
trifluoperazine (Stelazine)	10–60 mg daily
thioridazine (Melleril)	50–600 mg daily
fluphenazine decanoate (Modecate)	10–100 mg monthly by injection
butyrophenones:	
haloperidol (Haldol, Serenace)	10–80 mg daily
diphenylbutyl piperidines:	
pimozide (Orap)	2–12 mg daily
fluspirilene (Redeptin)	4–16 mg weekly by injection
thioxanthenes:	
flupenthixol decanoate (Depixol)	20–100 mg monthly by injection

It has been shown that these drugs act on the dopamine neurotransmitter system in the brain, a finding that has been used as provisional supportive evidence for the biochemical theories of schizophrenic disturbance, as described in Chapter 6. Acute schizophrenia remits far more quickly when treated with these drugs than without, even when the patient is treated in a well functioning psychiatric ward with proper attention and psychotherapy.

Once the force of the patient's hallucinations, delusions and bizarre thoughts has been diminished, and he becomes calmer, he is more readily accessible, so that staff and relatives are enabled to approach and understand him more easily.

The introduction of phenothiazine drugs, used widely from 1953 onwards, was a main factor in the achievement of better results, briefer periods in hospital, and fewer patients remaining in mental hospitals since that time. The number of inpatients (mainly schizophrenics) reached its maximum in many countries in the mid-1950s and has fallen ever since.

The drugs have disadvantages. With the larger doses, these include troublesome side-effects such as difficulty in coordinating movement, and gain in weight. These side-effects make the drugs unpopular with many of the patients, who may in any case be reluctant to take medication because it is prescribed medical treatment from doctors for an illness, the existence of which they firmly and vigorously deny. When the psychiatrists further recommend prolonged treatment even after apparent recovery, in order to reduce the likelihood of relapse, even more of the patients are reluctant, not to say evasive, about continuing on the drugs. The long-acting injections are used for greater reliability of dosage in these reluctant patients.

The evidence that the treatment with drugs is valuable and the main intervention to recommend in our present state of knowledge is plentiful and well based. In the first place it was founded on the clinical observations of psychiatrists who noted the improvement in disturbed patients (although there was much less effect on the withdrawal, apathy and lack of interest of the chronically disabled), and the frequent relapses of patients who stopped their medication after a time. Secondly, the evidence comes from scientific trials, of which four will be mentioned.

In England, Leff and Wing[129] studied the effect of medication on the prevention of relapse in patients who had recovered and were outpatients, comparing the drug tablets with neutral sugar tablets to control the effects of suggestibility. They found that the patients who had had acute illnesses and recovered well, so that their psychiatrists saw a good chance of sustained recovery, did not receive additional protection against relapse by being on medication. The patients who had had the most severe illnesses relapsed frequently with or without medication, so that it may have helped only some of them, and only slightly. However, an important group of patients with intermediate prognosis relapsed much less frequently when on the drug than when taking the neutral tablets.

In Boston, a study[68] compared the effect of drugs with that of psychotherapy and moving the patients from a traditional mental hospital, where the wards were backwaters, although work and occupational rehabilitation were available, to a busy research ward in a postgraduate hospital, with very active regimes, large numbers of staff per patient, and psychotherapy of a high standard. The patients were chronic schizophrenics who had spent several years of disability in hospital. Those who remained in the mental hospital appeared to do as well as those who were moved to the more stimulating ward regime, and the authors wondered if the patients in the 'better' hospital were sometimes overwhelmed and driven into relapse by the vigorous social stimulation provided. This is known to be harmful to many such chronic patients, and they also might have been at a disadvantage in not having access to the graded offers of paid work available in the traditional setting. The doctors concluded that, 'Psychotherapy in chronic schizophrenia seemed to add little of significance to clinical improvement unless associated with drug intake' and, indeed, treatment with drugs was usually necessary to enable the patient to start participating in psychotherapy and the more stimulating wards.[67]

In the studies of Hogarty and his colleagues on the effects of different kinds of follow-up treatment,[81,82] also carried out in the USA, the results in terms of keeping patients so well that they stayed out of hospital were particularly clear. They compared four regimes: drugs alone (with perfunctory personal attention in the outpatient clinic); drugs and good social work counselling; the same good counselling without any drugs; and perfunctory attention alone. The two drug regimes did best, drugs plus counselling being slightly more successful than drugs alone, and well behind came counselling without drugs, which was slightly better than nothing. In other words, drugs are much the more important measure in good after-care for schizophrenics (and when the patients allocated to drug regimes *did* relapse, it was often because they had stopped the drug against advice). The counselling helped modestly as well. Also in the United States, May's[150] project studying five different regimes in 228 new cases of moderately severe schizophrenia gave rather similar results after 5 years of treatment: the treatment involving drugs helped the patients most, and psychotherapy was not an important additional ingredient.

Broadly similar evidence on the interaction of physical and psychological measures, showing that they facilitate each other, is being collected at the Institute of Psychiatry, London.[225]

Electroconvulsive treatment

This treatment, effective and merciful in relieving the severest depressive illnesses, is much less helpful in most cases of schizophrenia. Nevertheless, it speeds up return to calmer normal states in severely disturbed, agitated patients, in those who are dangerously depressed at the same time as suffering schizophrenic experiences, and in the most withdrawn patients of all, who may be in physical danger from starvation and not drinking.[178],[217]

Functional neurosurgery (psychosurgery; formerly 'leucotomy')

In the 1940s and 1950s, when there was little relief available for the unremitting suffering of the worst cases of schizophrenia, neuro-surgeons and psychiatrists co-operated in devising operations to cut the tracts of the brain that subserve emotion, in an effort to mitigate severe tension and distress without damaging intellect or the person-ality as a whole. The operations were at first difficult to make reliable, so that while many schizophrenics were helped, some were made worse by side-effects of inaccurately placed cuts. Nowadays the improved treatment of schizophrenia with safe drugs has made surgical operations for its relief obsolete (the few – only 62 in 1980 – greatly improved and accurate psychosurgical operations carried out in Britain annually are now very largely for the relief of the severest depressive illnesses).[19]

Management of chronic schizophrenia in the mental hospital

Much has been learnt of the essentials of good treatment in mental hospitals since the days of neglected asylums described by Barton,[6] Goffman,[63] and Wing and Brown.[237] Open-door policies in previously closed institutions and effective drugs both date from the 1950s and have continued to be refined since then.

Both understimulation and overstimulation are harmful, the former leading to the apathetic and neglected state of the 'long-stay' patients in poor asylums, the latter precipitating defensive withdrawal and even the return of vivid hallucinations and disturbed behaviour. Enriching the deprived social environment requires giving the patients normal clothes, property and living space, opening the doors, letting patients of different sexes meet each other, encouraging visiting by relatives and volunteers, and holding social events in the hospital. Efforts to improve manners and behaviour may remove obstacles to the patient's ability to live outside hospital again. Experiments with wards in which the whole regime is adapted to teach and reward more natural and acceptable behaviour – the so-called token economy – have shown that the patients certainly learn to do better, although much of the improvement is only temporary. Some of the chronic patients are handicapped by slowness, poor concentration, lack of initiative and consequent inability to perform complicated tasks at their former level of achievement. The degree of these handicaps is at times extremely severe, to an extent known only to relatives, psychiatric nurses in the long-stay wards and some intrepid research workers who have lived with the patients in isolation.[152] Students fail to resume higher education, and skilled workers drift downwards in society and can no longer hold even unskilled jobs. Housewives fail to organise their households and cannot take an interest in or control their children. Part of the rehabilitative task of the hospital is to offer a variety of occupations and jobs, graded for interest, and paying money, to make the most of the remaining capacity of the patients and make them ready for return to life outside.

The trades involved in running the institution, working on the hospital farm, in the laundry and stores, gardening, and painting and decorating, have traditionally been offered to the long-term patients, no doubt partly as a form of economy in Victorian times and later, and to assure the guardians that the pauper inmates were in productive labour, but almost exclusively today as an offer of constructive and realistic return to normal working conditions. Industrial units for factory work and printing have been set up in many hospitals for this purpose, and many patients also take outside jobs and travel to them every day, using the hospital as a residential hostel in the final stages of their stay there. Classes are held to improve rusty skills in literacy, cooking, shopping, sewing and typing.

Social and domestic rehabilitation also proceeds by way of different social settings within the hospital. Some wards are run with an informal atmosphere: the nurses and occupational therapists do not wear uniform, and carry out cooking, shopping and other aspects of daily living with the patients. Staff and patients together discuss emotional problems, difficulties with personal relationships, practical problems, and how to start tackling them. Unstaffed flats have been furnished in the hospital grounds for the patients to practice independent existence before they leave altogether.

Management of chronic schizophrenia in the community

Many schizophrenic patients return home, whether or not they have recovered fully, but often home is not the most favourable setting for getting well and staying well. To any original family disturbances, all too often still unresolved and perhaps irresoluble, may be added resentment and recrimination over the bad times preceding the admission. The family resent the difficult behaviour they had to live with; the patient resents the lack of understanding he received and his despatch to hospital. It is not surprising that patients returning to more emotional and openly critical relatives relapse frequently, an observation familiar to clinicians and recently confirmed by the research of the Institute of Psychiatry.[225]

However, the empty life and isolation in bed-sitting rooms in landladies' houses also lead to deterioration. The patients sit for hours doing absolutely nothing, neglect to eat and keep clean, and become more withdrawn and mentally abnormal in their isolation. The right direction on the narrow path that the disabled patient must tread between over- and understimulation is best provided, if not in a hospital ward, by special hostels with counselling staff who have chosen this kind of work. This placement often seems to be right for the individual patient, and research confirms a lower relapse rate in hostels.[21]

Efforts to help the patient spend his time more productively are important. Attendance at day hospitals with occupational and social therapy, and at day centres where the patient is assured of a welcome, and can be given counselling and occupation for wages, is helpful. Sheltered employment may be needed for those who remain at a disadvantage on the open market for work. This will include assembly work in factories for the unskilled, non-manual posts in clerical work, and filing and cataloguing for students who have to accept that they cannot pursue higher education after all.

Because the drugs help to prevent relapse, and can exert some protection even when patients return to disturbed families,[225] many of the patients are best advised to continue taking medication for a substantial period after the last period of acute illness. Unfortunately, stopping the drugs after a few years of apparent health, or at least freedom from active symptoms, is not always safe, as relapses in the succeeding few weeks are common.[82]

The families feel burdened, ill understood by the professional services, and bewildered by the patients' behaviour. They have in the past been offered little help except the admission of the patient when life was intolerable, and now the emphasis on community care outside institutions means that disturbed patients remain at home while the supposed care may be scanty. Informed advice about illness and its disabilities, about social over- and understimulation and reducing the intensity and duration of contact within the family when the patient's condition shows signs of relapse, about the drugs and about the services available, has been lacking and sorely missed.[38]

Counselling of patient, relatives and family as a whole may be provided by social workers, psychiatrists in outpatient clinics, and particularly by community psychiatric nurses, who have unrivalled knowledge of the condition as seen in its severe form in hospital, and are now increasingly working with patients and families at home. Further support for the families may be available by way of self-help groups that exchange information and advice, especially the National Schizophrenia Fellowship.*

It is now clear from the long-term studies of the fate of patients diagnosed decades ago as suffering from undoubted schizophrenia, that the prospects are not so bad as used to be thought. These studies,[15, 26] mentioned in Chapter 3, show that even before the present-day drugs, open hospitals and community services became available, half of the patients made substantial recoveries completely or nearly to their old selves. The mild problems that remained in some of these patients were not so much mental abnormalities like hallucinations, as problems in social adaptation: peculiar habits and appearance, or an unacceptably cavalier attitude to others' feelings. Modern methods of treatment certainly help considerably during the acute illness and for a few years thereafter: whether there is longer-lasting benefit greater than that of a few years ago is uncertain, but a reasonable hope.

The problem is not only to treat the illness, the gross, out-of-control mental abnormalities, as we can do with drugs, admission and imaginative general care, but then to devise methods of reaching healthy aspects of the person that are preserved, but in retreat, far inside.

The treatment has improved greatly, and is still improving. Yet, as schizophrenia is a severe disability, treatment after its onset can never be expected to achieve brilliant results. We need to be better at prevention, which has not been mentioned in this book because we scarcely know how to begin. It is because prevention and better treatment can only be based on more knowledge, and because speculation and research will have to start from the present stock of knowledge, that I have written this book about what we know – or think we know – now.

* 29 Victoria Road, Surbiton, Surrey KT6 4JT.

References

1   Allderidge, P. 1979. Hospitals, madhouses and asylums: cycles in the care of the insane. *Br. J. Psychiat.* **134**, 321–34.
2   Arieti, S. 1974. *Interpretation of schizophrenia,* 2nd edn. London: Crosby Lockwood Staples.
3   Ibid., 81–2.
4   Ibid., 501–2.
5   Barnes, M. and J. Berke 1971. *Mary Barnes: two accounts of a journey through madness.* London: MacGibbon & Kee.
6   Barton, R. 1966. *Institutional neurosis,* 2nd edn. Bristol: John Wright.
7   Bastide, R. 1972. *The sociology of mental disorder,* 200, 201, 206 (transl. J. McNeil). London: Routledge & Kegan Paul.
8   Ibid., 218–9.
9   Bateson, G. (ed.) 1962. *Perceval's narrative: a patient's account of his psychosis 1830–1832,* xi, xix. London: Hogarth Press.
10 Bateson, G., D. Jackson, J. Haley and J. Weakland 1956. Toward a theory of schizophrenia. *Behav. Sci.* **1**, 251–64.
11 Becker, H. S. 1963. *Outsiders: studies in the sociology of deviance.* New York: Free Press.
12 Benedict, R. Quoted in Rosen (1968),[171] op. cit., 55.
13 Birley, J. L. T. and G. W. Brown 1970. Crises and life changes preceding the onset or relapse of acute schizophrenia: clinical aspects. *Br. J. Psychiat.* **116**, 327–33.
14 Bleuler, E. 1911. *Dementia praecox or the group of schizophrenias.* (transl. J. Zinkin 1951). London: George Allen & Unwin.
15 Bleuler, M. 1978. *The schizophrenic disorders: long-term patient and family studies,* 497, 500 (transl. S. M. Clemens from German edn 1972). New Haven: Yale University Press.
16 Bleuler, M. 1972. In *Psychiatrie der Gegenwart, Forschung und Praxis,* K. P. Kisker *et al.* (eds), 2nd edn, Book II, Part I, 9–17. Berlin: Springer.
17 Böök, J. A. 1953. A genetic and neuropsychiatric investigation of a North-Swedish population. *Acta Genet.* (Basle) **4**, 1.
18 Bowra, C. M. 1944. *Sophoclean tragedy,* paperback edn 1965, 31. Oxford: Oxford University Press.
19 Bridges, P. K. and J. R. Bartlett 1973. The work of a psychosurgical unit. *Postgrad. Med. J.* **49**, 855–9.
20 Brown, G. W., J. L. T. Birley and J. K. Wing 1972. Influence of family life on the course of schizophrenic disorders: a replication. *Br. J. Psychiat.* **121**, 241–58.
21 Brown, G. W., M. Bone, B. Dalison and J. K. Wing 1966. *Schizophrenia and social care.* Oxford: Oxford University Press.
22 Brown, L. B. 1980. A psychologist's perspective on psychiatry in China. *Aust. N.Z. J. Psychiat.* **14**, 21–35.
23 Burton, R. 1621. *Anatomy of melancholy,* H. Jackson (ed.). London: Dent, 1932.
24 Cawte, J. E. 1965. Ethnopsychiatry in Central Australia – I. 'Traditional' illnesses in the Eastern Aranda people. *Br. J. Psychiat.* **111**, 1069–77.
25 Cawte, J. E. and M. A. Kidson 1965. Ethnopsychiatry in Central Australia – II. The evolution of illness in a Walbiri lineage. *Br. J. Psychiat.* **111**, 1079–85.

26 Ciompi, L. 1980. The natural history of schiozphrenia in the long term. *Br. J. Psychiat.* **136,** 413–20.

27 Clarke, B. 1975. *Mental disorder in earlier Britain,* 69. Cardiff: University of Wales Press.

28 Ibid., 79.

29 Ibid., 81.

30 Ibid., 92.

31 Ibid., 151–75.

32 Ibid., 176–206.

33 Cohn, N. 1976. *Europe's inner demons: an enquiry inspired by the great witch-hunt,* 262. London: Paladin.

34 Connell, P. H. 1958. *Amphetamine psychosis.* London: Chapman & Hall.

35 Conolly, J. 1849. Croonian lectures on some of the forms of insanity. *Lancet* **(ii),** 357, 414.

36 Cooper, B. 1978. Epidemiology. In *Schizophrenia: towards a new synthesis,* J. K. Wing (ed.), 31–51. London: Academic Press.

37 Cooper, J. E., R. E. Kendell, B. J. Gurland *et al.* 1972. *Psychiatric diagnosis in New York and London.* Oxford: Oxford University Press.

38 Creer, C. 1978. Social work with patients and their families. In *Schizophrenia: towards a new synthesis,* J. K. Wing (ed.), 233–51. London: Academic Press.

39 Crider, A. 1979. *Schizophrenia: a biopsychological perspective,* 146. Chichester: Wiley.

40 Davison, K. and C. R. Bagley 1969. Schizophrenia-like psychoses associated with organic disorders of the central nervous system: a review of the literature. In *Current problems in neuropsychiatry,* R. N. Herrington (ed.). *Br. J. Psychiat.* Special Publication no. 4, 113–84.

41 Department of Health and Social Security 1979. *Inpatient statistics from the Mental Health Enquiry for England, 1976.* London: HMSO.

42 Dieckhofer, K. 1975. Lope de Vegas Komödie 'Los locos de Valencia' – ein kultur-historischer Einblick in eine psychiatrische Anstalt des 15. Jahrhunderts. *Schweiz. Arch. Neurol. Neurochirurgie Psychiat.* **116,** 343–51.

43 Dostoyevsky, F. 1866. *Crime and punishment* (transl. D. Magarshack). London: Penguin, 1951.

44 Ducey, C. and B. Simon 1975. Ancient Greece and Rome. In *World history of psychiatry,* J. G. Howells (ed.), 1–38. London: Baillière Tindall.

45 Dunham, H. W. 1976. Society, culture and mental disorder. *Archs Gen. Psychiat.* **33,** 147–56.

46 Edgar, I. I. 1970. *Shakespeare, medicine and psychiatry,* 190. New York: Vision Press.

47 Edwards, J. H. 1972. The genetical basis of schizophrenia. In *Genetic factors in 'Schizophrenia',* A. R. Kaplan (ed.), 310–14. Springfield Ill.: C. C. Thomas.

48 Ellmann, R. 1959. *James Joyce,* 692. Oxford: Oxford University Press.

49 Elnagar, M. N., P. Maitra and M. N. Rao 1971. Mental health in an Indian rural community. *Br. J. Psychiat.* **118,** 499–503.

50 Esterson, A. 1970. *The leaves of spring.* London: Tavistock. (paperback edn London: Penguin, 1972.)

51 Ezekiel, *passim,* especially Chs 1–5 and 14, i–ii.

52 Farber, L. 1972. In *Laing and anti-psychiatry,* R. Boyers & R. Orrill (eds), 171. London: Penguin.

53 Festinger, L., H. Riecken and S. Schachter 1956. *When prophecy fails.* Minneapolis: University of Minnesota Press.

54 Field, M. J. 1960. *The search for security: an ethnopsychiatric study of rural Ghana,* 215. London: Faber & Faber.

55 Ibid., 455, 460, 462, 467.

56   Foucault, M. 1967. *Madness and civilization*, xiv, 39, 121. London: Tavistock.
57   Freeman, H. 1978. Pharmacological treatment and management. In *Schizophrenia: towards a new synthesis*, J. K. Wing (ed.), 167–87. London: Academic Press.
58   Freud, S. 1911. *Psycho-analytic notes upon an autobiographical account of a case of paranoia (dementia paranoides)*, standard edn, vol. 12, 3. London: Hogarth. (Paperback edn Pelican Freud Library, vol. 9, 129–223: London: Penguin, 1979.)
59   Friedhoff, A. J. and E. van Winkle 1962. The characteristics of an amine found in the urine of schizophrenic patients. *J. Nerv. Ment. Dis.* **135**, 550–5.
60   Fromm-Reichmann, F. 1948. Notes on the development of treatment of schizophrenia by psychoanalytic psychotherapy. *Psychiatry* **11**, 263–73.
61   George, K. M. 1963. Pinel or Chiarugi? *Med. Hist.* **7**, 371–80.
62   German, G. A. 1972. Aspects of clinical psychiatry in sub-Saharan Africa, *Br. J. Psychiat.* **121**, 461–79.
63   Goffman, E. 1961. *Asylums: essays on the social situation of mental patients and other inmates.* Garden City, NY: Anchor Press.
64   Ibid., 379–80, 384.
65   Goldhamer, H. and A. Marshall 1963. *Psychosis and Civilisation.* Glencoe, Ill.: Free Press.
66   Green, H. 1964. *I never promised you a rose garden.* London: Gollancz. (Paperback edn Pan 1967.)
67   Greenblatt, M. 1972. Preface. In *Schizophrenia: pharmacotherapy and psychotherapy*, L. Grinspoon, J. R. Ewalt & R. I. Shader, x. Baltimore: Williams & Wilkins.
68   Grinspoon, L., J. R. Ewalt and R. I. Shader 1972. *Schizophrenia: pharmacotherapy and psychotherapy.* Baltimore: Williams & Wilkins.
69   Hare, E. H. 1978. Variations in the seasonal distribution of births of psychotic patients in England and Wales. *Br. J. Psychiat.* **132**, 155–8.
70   Hasenfus, N. and P. Magaro 1976. Creativity and schizophrenia: an equality of empirical constructs. *Br. J. Psychiat.* **129**, 346–9.
71   Haslam, J. 1810. *Illustrations of madness: exhibiting a singular case of insanity, and a no less remarkable difference in medical opinion: developing the nature of assailment, and the manner of working events; with a description of the tortures experienced by bomb-bursting, lobster-cracking and lengthening the brain. Embellished by a curious plate.* London: Hayden. (See Leigh 1961[131].)
72   Hemmings, G. and W. A. Hemmings (eds) 1978. *The biological basis of schizophrenia.* Baltimore: University Park Press.
73   Herodotus *c.* 480–425 BC. See Rosen (1968).[171]
74   Heston, L. L. 1966. Psychiatric disorders in foster home reared children of schizophrenic mothers. *Br. J. Psychiat.* **112**, 819–25.
75   Hill, C. 1975. *The world turned upside down.* London: Penguin.
76   Hill. R. G. 1839. *A lecture on the management of lunatic asylums.* London: Simpkin Marshall.
77   Ibid., 4–5. (Quoted in Scull 1979, p. 95.[190])
78   Hinsie, L. E. and R. J. Campbell 1970. *Psychiatric dictionary*, 4th edn. New York: Oxford University Press.
79   Hippocrates *c.* 430–330 BC. *Hippocratic writings*, G. E. R. Lloyd (ed.). London: Penguin, 1978.
80   Hirsch, S. R. and J. P. Leff 1975. *Abnormalities in parents of schizophrenics.* Oxford: Oxford University Press.
81   Hogarty, G. E. and S. C. Goldberg 1973. Drug and sociotherapy in the aftercare of schizophrenic patients. *Archs Gen. Psychiat.* **28**, 54–64.
82   Hogarty, G. E., R. F. Ulrich, F. Mussare and N. Aristigueta 1976. Drug discon-

tinuation among long-term successfully maintained schizophrenic outpatients. *Dis. Nerv. Syst.* **37,** 494–500.

83   Hunter, R. and I. Macalpine 1964. *Three hundred years of psychiatry 1535–1860,* 6. Oxford: Oxford University Press.

84   Ibid., 154–7.

85   Ibid., 358.

86   Ibid., 405–6.

87   Hunter, R. and I. Macalpine 1974. *Psychiatry for the poor: 1851 Colney Hatch Asylum; Friern Hospital 1973.* London: Dawson.

88   Ibid., 86.

89   Ibid., 109.

90   Iversen, L. L. 1978. Biochemical and pharmacological studies. In *Schizophrenia: towards a new synthesis* J. K. Wing (ed.), 89–116. London: Academic Press.

91   James, W. 1902. *The varieties of religious experience,* 35. London: Fontana, 1960.

92   Ibid., 88.

93   Ibid., 330.

94   Jones, K. 1972. *A history of the Mental Health Services.* London: Routledge & Kegan Paul.

95   Ibid., 64.

96   Ibid., 70.

97   Ibid., 120–1.

98   Ibid., 181.

99   Ibid., 357.

100 Jung, C. G. 1976. *Letters,* G. Adler (ed.), vol. 2, 266 (transl. R. F. C. Hull). London: Routledge & Kegan Paul.

101 Kanner, L. 1949. Problems of nosology and psychodynamics of early infantile autism. *Am. J. Orthopsychiat.* **19,** 416–26.

102 Kety, S. S. 1975. Quoted in *American psychiatry: past present and future,* G. Kreigman *et al.* (eds), 117. Virginia: Virginia University Press.

103 Kety, S. S. 1980. The syndrome of schizophrenia: unresolved questions and opportunities for research. *Br. J. Psychiat.* **136,** 421–36.

104 Kety, S. S., D. Rosenthal, P. H. Wender, *et al.* 1975. In *Genetic research in psychiatry* R. R. Fieve, D. Rosenthal & H. Brill (eds), 147–65. Baltimore: Johns Hopkins University Press.

105 Kraepelin, E. 1913. *Psychiatrie – ein Lehrbuch für Studierende und Ärzte,* 8th edn. Leipzig: Barth. (The section on 'Endogenous dementias' publ. as *Dementia praecox and paraphrenia,* G. M. Robertson (ed.) (transl. R. M. Barclay). Edinburgh: Livingstone, 1919. This was the source used by the author.)

106 Ibid., 1, 3, 10.

107 Kroll, J. 1973. A reappraisal of psychiatry in the Middle Ages. *Archs Gen. Psychiat.* **29,** 276–83.

108 Kulhara, P. and N. N. Wig 1978. The chronicity of schizophrenia in North West India. *Br. J. Psychiat.* **132,** 186–90.

109 Laing, R. D. 1961. *The self and others.* London: Tavistock.

110 Laing, R. D. 1965. *The divided self.* London: Penguin. (Originally Chicago: Quadrangle Books, 1960.)

111 Ibid., Preface.

112 Ibid., 9.

113 Ibid., 27, 29, 30, 33, 36.

114 Ibid., e.g. 27, 28, 34, 36, 50, Ch. 9.

115 Ibid., 140, 147–8.

116 Ibid., 164.

117 Ibid., 178 ff.

118   Laing, R. D. 1967. *The politics of experience*. London: Penguin.
119   Ibid., 11–12.
120   Ibid., 86.
121   Ibid., 95, 96, 98, 100.
122   Ibid., 105, 110, 114.
123   Ibid., 136.
124   Laing, R. D. 1971. *Knots*, 1, 5. London: Penguin.
125   Ibid., 56.
126   Laing, R. D. and A. Esterson 1964. *Sanity, madness and the family*, 1. London: Tavistock.
127   Leff, J. 1978. Social and psychological causes of the acute attack. In *Schizophrenia: towards a new synthesis*, J. F. Wing (ed.) 139–65. London: Academic Press.
128   Leff, J. and C. Vaughn 1980. The interaction of life events and relatives' expressed emotion in schizophrenia and depressive neurosis. *Br. J. Psychiat.* **136**, 146–53.
129   Leff, J. P. and J. K. Wing 1971. Trial of maintenance therapy in schizophrenia. *Br. Med. J.* **iii**, 599–604.
130   Lehmann, H. 1966. In *Psychopathology of schizophrenia*, P. Hoch & J. Zubin (eds). New York: Grune & Stratton. Quoted in Venables, 226, p. 128.
131   Leigh, D. 1961. *The historical development of British psychiatry*, vol. I, *18th and 19th century*. Oxford: Pergamon.
132   Ibid., 241, 244.
133   Lemert, E. 1951. *Social pathology*. New York: McGraw-Hill.
134   Lemert, E. 1967. *Human deviance, social problems and social control*. Englewood Cliffs, NJ: Prentice-Hall.
135   Lidz, T. 1972. Schizophrenia, R. D. Laing and the contemporary treatment of psychosis. In *Laing and anti-psychiatry*, R. Boyers & R. Orrill (eds), 123–156 (see especially 141, 147). London: Penguin.
136   Lidz, T. 1975. *The origin and treatment of schizophrenic disorders*. London: Hutchinson.
137   Ibid., 53.
138   Ibid., 70.
139   Ibid., 113.
140   Linton, R. 1956. In *Culture and mental disorders*, G. Devereux (ed.). Springfield, Ill.: C. C. Thomas.
141   Liu, X. 1980. Mental health work in Sichuan. *Br. J. Psychiat.* **137**, 371–6.
142   Locke, J. 1978. *An essay concerning human understanding*, edited with an introduction by J. W. Yolton. London: Dent (Everyman).
143   Macalpine, I. and R. Hunter 1966. The 'insanity' of King George III: a classic case of porphyria. *Br. Med. J.* **i**, 65–71.
144   Macalpine, I. and R. Hunter 1968. Porphyria in the royal houses of Stuart, Hanover and Prussia. *Br. Med. J.* **i**, 7–18.
145   Macalpine, I. and R. Hunter 1969. *George III and the mad-business*. London: Allen Lane Penguin.
146   Macfarlane, A. 1970. *Witchcraft in Tudor and Stuart England*. London: Routledge & Kegan Paul.
147   McGhie, A. and J. Chapman 1961. Disorders of attention and perception in early schizophrenia. *Br. J. Med. Psychol.* **34**, 103–16.
148   McWhirter, N. (ed.) 1979. *Guinness book of records*, 176. London: Guinness Superlatives.
149   Malzberg, B. 1956. *Migration and mental disease: a study of first admissions to hospitals for mental disease, New York, 1939–41*. New York: Social Science Research Council.

150   May, P. R. A., A. H. Tuma and W. J. Dixon 1976. Schizophrenia: a follow-up study of results of treatment. *Archs Gen. Psychiat.* **33**, 474–8, 481–6.

151   Mellor, C. S. 1970. First-rank symptoms of schizophrenia. *Br. J. Psychiat.* **117**, 15–23.

152   Morgan, R. 1977. Three weeks in isolation with two chronic schizophrenic patients. *Br. J. Psychiat.* **131**, 504–13.

153   Murphy, H. B. M. and A. C. Raman 1971. The chronicity of schizophrenia in indigenous tropical peoples. *Br. J. Psychiat.* **118**, 489–97.

154   Murphy, J. M. 1976. Psychiatric labelling in cross-cultural perspective. *Science* **191**, 1019–28.

155   Neki, J. S. 1973. Psychiatry in South-East Asia. *Br. J. Psychiat.* **123**, 257–69.

156   Neugebauer, R. 1979. Mediaeval and early modern theories of mental illness. *Archs Gen. Psychiat.* **36**, 477–83.

157   Newman, J. H. 1864. *Apologia pro vita sua.* London: Dent, 1912.

158   Paracelsus (Theophrastus von Hohenheim) 1567. Quoted in Mora, G. 1967. 'Paracelsus' psychiatry: on the occasion of the 400th anniversary of his book *Diseases that deprive man of his reason. Am. J. Psychiat.* **124**, 803–14.

159   Parry-Jones, W. L. 1972. *The trade in lunacy: a study of private madhouses in England in the eighteenth and nineteenth centuries.* London: Routledge & Kegan Paul.

160   Pascal, B. 1670. *Pensées,* iv, 277 (transl. A. J. Krailsheimer). London: Penguin, 1970.

161   Pinel, P. 1806. *A treatise on insanity* (transl. D. D. Davis). Sheffield. New York: Hafner, 1962.

162   Pirsig, R. M. 1974. *Zen and the art of motorcycle maintenance.* London: The Bodley Head. (Paperback edn Corgi, 1976.)

163   Plato 427—348 BC. *Phaedrus,* 244–5.

164   Plato 427–348 BC. *Republic,* 588B–589A.

165   Post, F. 1966. *Persistent persecutory states of the elderly.* London: Pergamon.

166   Pritchard, M. J. 1967. Prognosis of schizophrenia before and after pharmaco-therapy. *Br. J. Psychiat.* **113**, 1345–52; 1353–9.

167   Raman, A. C. and H. B. M. Murphy 1972. Failure of traditional prognostic indicators in Afro-Asian psychotics: results of a long-term follow up survey. *J. Nerv. Ment. Dis.* **154**, 238–47.

168   Report of the Resident Physician of Hanwell Asylum 1842. See Leigh (1961), op. cit.,[131] 222.

169   Roper, W. 1626. *A man of singular virtue,* A. L. Rowse (ed.). London: Folio Society, 1980.

170   Rosen, G. 1967. Emotion and sensibility in ages of anxiety: a comparative historical review. *Am. J. Psychiat.* **124**, 771–84.

171   Rosen, G. 1968. *Madness in society.* London: Routledge & Kegan Paul.

172   Ibid., Ch. 2, 21–70.

173   Ibid., 37.

174   Ibid., 58–9.

175   Ibid., 94–5, 97.

176   Ibid., 104, 106.

177   Rosenhan, D. 1973. On being sane in insane places. *Science* **179**, 250–8.

178   Royal College of Psychiatrists 1977. Memorandum on the use of electroconvulsive therapy. *Br. J. Psychiat.* **131**, 261–72.

179   1. *Samuel,* Ch. 10, verses x–xi; Ch. 15, verses xxvii–xxx; Ch. 21, verse xiii; Ch. 28, verses vii–xxv; Ch. 31, verses i–vi.

180   Schatzman, M. 1973. *Soul murder: persecution in the family.* London: Allen Lane Penguin.

181 Ibid., 11.
182 Ibid., 30–1, 33–41, 46–7.
183 Scheff, T. J. 1966. *Being mentally ill – a sociological theory*, 25, 28, 33–4. London: Weidenfeld & Nicolson.
184 Ibid., 149.
185 Schneider, K. 1950. *Klinische Psychopathologie*. Stuttgart: Thieme. (American edn *Clinical psychopathology*, 133–4 (transl. M. W. Hamilton). New York: Grune & Stratton, 1959.)
186 Schreber, D. P. 1955. *Memoirs of my nervous illness* (transl. I. Macalpine & R. Hunter (also eds)). London: Dawson.
187 Ibid., 99, 112, 119.
188 Ibid., 320.
189 Scott, R. D. 1976. 'Closure' in family relationships and the first official diagnosis. In *Schizophrenia 75: psychotherapy, family studies, research*, J. Jørstad & E. Ugelstad (eds), 265–81. Oslo: Universitets Forlaget.
190 Scull, A. T. 1979. *Museums of madness: the social organization of insanity in nineteenth-century England*. London: Allen Lane Penguin.
191 Ibid., 66.
192 Ibid., 92.
193 Ibid., 224, 247, 250–1.
194 Searles, H. F. 1959. The effort to drive the other crazy – an element in the aetiology & psychotherapy of schizophrenia. *Br. J. Med. Psychol.* **32**, 1–18. (Reprinted in *Collected papers on schizophrenia and allied subjects*, 254–83. London: Hogarth, 1965.)
195 Sechehaye, M. 1956. *A new psychotherapy in schizophrenia* (transl. G. Rubin-Rabson). New York: Grune and Stratton.
196 Seeman, P., T. Lee, M. Chau-Wong and K. Wong 1976. Antipsychotic drug doses and neuroleptic/dopamine receptors. *Nature* **261**, 717–9.
197 Shakespeare, W. 1623. *Merchant of Venice*, Act III, scene 2.
198 Shields, J. 1978. Genetics. In *Schizophrenia: towards a new synthesis*, J. K. Wing (ed.), 53–87. London: Academic Press.
199 Siegler, M., H. Osmond and H. Mann 1969. Laing's models of madness. *Br. J. Psychiat.* **115**, 947–58. (see *Laing and anti-psychiatry*, R. Boyers & R. Orrill (eds), 99–122. London: Penguin, 1972.)
200 Simon, B. 1978. *Mind and madness in Ancient Greece*. Ithaca and London: Cornell University Press.
201 Singer, M. T. and L. C. Wynne 1966. Communication styles in parents of normals, neurotics and schizophrenics. *Psychiat. Res. Rep.* **20**, 25–38.
202 Singer, M. T., L. C. Wynne and M. L. Toohey 1978. *Communication disorders and the families of schizophrenics*. In Wynne *et al.* (1978), op. cit.,[242] 499–511.
203 Slater, E., A. W. Beard, and E. Glithero 1963. The schizophrenia-like psychoses of epilepsy. *Br. J. Psychiat.* **109**, 95–150.
204 Slater, E. and M. Roth 1977. *Clinical psychiatry*, 3rd edn (rev.), 261. London: Baillière Tindall.
205 Smith, A. C. 1967. Clinical notes on Pinel's treatise on insanity. *Br. J. Med. Psychol.* **40**, 85–99.
206 Smith, A. C. 1968. Notes on difficulties defining delusion. *Br. J. Med. Psychol.* **41**, 255–9.
207 Snezhnevsky, A. V. 1971. The symptomatology, clinical forms and nosology of schizophrenia. In *Modern perspectives in world psychiatry*, J. G. Howells (ed.), 423–47. New York: Brunner/Mazel.
208 Speller, S. R. 1964. *The Mental Health Act, 1959*. London: Institute of Hospital Administrators.

209   Stafford-Clark, D. and A. C. Smith 1978. *Psychiatry for students,* 5th edn, 93, 95. London: George Allen & Unwin.
210   Storr, A. 1972. *The dynamics of creation,* esp. 50–74. London: Secker & Warburg.
211   Sullivan, H. S. 1956. *Clinical studies in psychiatry,* 367–88. New York: Norton.
212   Szasz, T. S. 1962. *The myth of mental illness.* London: Secker & Warburg.
213   Ibid., 59, 82.
214   Szasz, T. S. 1971. *The manufacture of madness.* London: Routledge & Kegan Paul.
215   Ibid., 65, 267, 278–9.
216   Taylor, F. K. 1966. *Psychopathology – its causes and symptoms,* 125–35. London: Butterworth.
217   Taylor, P. and J. J. Fleminger 1980. ECT for schizophrenia. *Lancet* **i,** 1380–3.
218   Tertullian, Q. S. F. *c.* 200. *De Carne Christi* (ii), 5.
219   Thomas, K. 1971. *Religion and the decline of magic: studies in popular beliefs in sixteenth and seventeenth century England.* London: Weidenfeld & Nicolson.
220   Torrey, E. F. 1979. Epidemiology. In *Disorders of the schizophrenic syndrome,* L. Bellak (ed.), 25–34. New York: Basic Books.
221   Trench, C. C. 1964. *The royal malady.* London: Longman.
222   Trevor-Roper, H. R. 1969. *The European witch-craze of the 16th and 17th centuries,* 120. London: Penguin.
223   Trilling, L. 1972. Mind in the modern world. In *Times Literary Supplement,* 17 November, 1381–5.
224   Tuke, S. 1813. *A description of the Retreat.* London: Dawson.
225   Vaughn, C. E. and J. P. Leff 1976. The influence of family & social factors in the course of psychiatric illness. *Br. J. Psychiat.* **129,** 125–37.
226   Venables, P. H. 1978. Cognitive disorder. In *Schizophrenia: towards a new synthesis,* J. K. Wing (ed.), 117–37. London: Academic Press.
227   Venables, P. H. and J. K. Wing 1962. Level of arousal and the subclassification of schizophrenia. *Archs Gen. Psychiat.* **7,** 114–19.
228   Watt, N. F. 1978. Patterns of childhood social development in adult schizophrenia. *Archs Gen. Psychiat.* **35,** 160–70.
229   Wender, P. H., D. Rosenthal, S. S. Kety, F. Schulsinger and J. Welner 1974. Cross-fostering. *Archs Gen. Psychiat.* **30,** 121–8.
230   West, D. J. and A. Walk 1977. *Daniel McNaughton: his trial and the aftermath.* Ashford, Kent; Headley Bros.
231   Whitwell, J. R. 1936. *Historical notes on psychiatry,* 32–4. London: H. K. Lewis.
232   Wilson, C. 1956. *The outsider.* London: Gollancz.
233   Wing, J. K. 1978. *Reasoning about madness.* 98–9, 138, 151. Oxford: Oxford University Press.
234   Ibid., 167–93.
235   Wing, J. K. (ed.) 1978. *Schizophrenia – towards a new synthesis.* London: Academic Press.
236   Ibid., 42–3.
237   Wing, J. K. and G. W. Brown 1970. *Institutionalism and Schizophrenia.* London: Cambridge University Press.
238   Wittkower, E. D. and R. Prince 1974. A review of transcultural psychiatry. In *American handbook of psychiatry,* S. Arieti (ed.), 2nd edn. New York: Basic Books.
239   Wolff, S. and J. Chick 1980. Schizoid personality in childhood: a controlled follow-up study. *Psychol. Med.* **10,** 85–100.
240   World Health Organisation 1973. *Report of the International Pilot Study of Schizophrenia,* vol. I. Geneva: WHO.
241   World Health Organisation 1979. *Schizophrenia – an international follow-up study.* Chichester: John Wiley.

242 Wynne, L. C., R. L. Cromwell and S. Matthysse 1978. *The nature of schizo-phrenia – new approaches to research and treatment.* New York: John Wiley.
243 Zilboorg, G. 1941. *A history of medical psychology,* 45. London: George Allen & Unwin.

Further reading: the best access to the facts on schizophrenia in one volume is in 242 above. Also strongly recommended: 15.

Index